SHAKESPEARE

HUTCHINSON'S UNIVERSITY LIBRARY

ENGLISH LITERATURE

EDITOR:

PROFESSOR BASIL WILLEY

M.A., F.B.A., HON.LITT.D.

*King Edward VII Professor of English Literature in the
University of Cambridge*

SHAKESPEARE

by

GEORGE IAN DUTHIE

M.A., PH.D., D.LITT.

MOLSON PROFESSOR OF ENGLISH,
MCGILL UNIVERSITY, MONTREAL.
LATE LECTURER IN ENGLISH IN
THE UNIVERSITY OF EDINBURGH

1951
HUTCHINSON'S UNIVERSITY LIBRARY
Hutchinson House, London, W.1.

New York   *Melbourne*   *Sydney*   *Cape Town*

Printed in Great Britain
at the Gainsborough Press, St. Albans,
by Fisher, Knight and Co. Ltd.

CONTENTS

FOREWORD

IF I were asked to name one or two introductory books suitable for the general reader who wishes to study Shakespeare, I should begin by suggesting Sir Edmund Chambers's *Shakespeare: A Survey*, Professor G. B. Harrison's *Introducing Shakespeare*, and Professor Dover Wilson's *The Essential Shakespeare*, and I should go on to say that there are legions of other books from among which he can select further reading. The present little volume is not intended to vie with any of the books just named. I have concentrated on only a limited number of Shakespeare's plays, and I have discussed these from certain special points of view. In particular, I have throughout concerned myself a great deal with the matter which forms the subject of Chapter II. Indeed, as far as the bulk of the book is concerned, it might well have been entitled *The Order Theme in Shakespeare*.

The scope of the book is limited, then. Some of the plays— even some of the finest—are not discussed; and those that are discussed are not considered in full detail in all their aspects. Furthermore, I should not like to make any claims for this work on the score of originality. Much that I say has been said before, whether frequently or infrequently. I have tried to acknowledge all my debts: but, if some have escaped my awareness as I wrote, I apologize.

Finally, I should like to record my gratitude to the McGill University Committee on Research, which made me a generous monetary grant which defrayed certain expenses involved in the preparation of my manuscript for the press.

G. I. D.

CHAPTER I

SHAKESPEARE'S CHARACTERS AND TRUTH TO LIFE

ONE of the statements most commonly made in praise of Shakespeare is that he is a creator of characters in which the spectator or reader can believe as if they were actual flesh-and-blood human beings existing in the real world of men and women. On the other hand, there are critics who maintain that to approach a Shakespeare play expecting this is a mistake. It has been claimed by some that the characters we encounter in Shakespeare, and the situations, are not in all cases such as we should be likely to encounter in real life.

One of the best known of American writers on Shakespeare, Professor Elmer Edgar Stoll, speaking not of Shakespeare alone, goes so far as to say[1] that "in the greatest tragedies (and comedies and epics too) the situation has been fundamentally improbable, unreasonable." "What are the greatest stories in the world?" he goes on to ask. "Those of Orestes, Oedipus, Achilles, and Odysseus; of Iphigeneia, Dido, Phaedra, Medea, and Herod and Mariamne; of Tristram and Isolt, Siegfried and Brünnhilde; of the Cid, Faustus, and Don Juan; of Lear, Othello, Macbeth, and Hamlet: all of them embodying situations improbable to an extreme degree. Their improbability," he continues, "is the price of their effectiveness: such fine and fruitful situations life itself does not afford."

Now this is a very sweeping statement—that all the greatest stories in the world's literature are fundamentally improbable, unreasonable. We are concerned here only with

[1] All quotations from Professor Stoll given in this chapter are from Chapters I and II of his *Art and Artifice in Shakespeare* (1934).

Shakespeare, and it will be well to look rather carefully at Professor Stoll's criticism of Shakespeare. Our space is limited, and we can deal with only one play. I choose *Othello*, because Professor Stoll calls it "the crucial case." "Here," he declares, speaking of *Othello*, "in its most complete and fruitful, but also most improbable, form, is the situation as I conceive of it; and the relation of character to action; and the supremacy of dramatic effect and illusion over both."

According to Professor Stoll, *Othello* is a play concerning a hero who, as a result of suggestions made to him by a villain, becomes thoroughly jealous; but before the villain began to make these suggestions the hero was *not* of a jealous nature— the reverse. That is to say, "the hero . . . is a prey to passions foreign (in a sense) to his nature, and is led into conduct to which he is not inclined." "There can be no question," says Professor Stoll, "for those who either heed the text or hearken to critical authority, of Othello's lacking the jealous nature before temptation, and being jealous thereupon without it; and only the transition causes difficulty."

Stoll holds that the transition is non-realistic—it is not true to life: Shakespeare did not mean it to be true to life, and he knew what he was doing. According to the psychological probabilities of real life, a man who reacted as Othello does to Iago's insinuations—so immediately, so passionately—would be a man naturally disposed to jealousy, which Othello is not. According to the psychological probabilities of real life, a man free from any disposition to jealousy—as Othello is shown by Shakespeare to be before the temptation—would not react to Iago's initial insinuations as Othello does. Othello falls a very ready victim to Iago's hints. Stoll declares that "Othello is made to believe a man whom he has officially slighted, and with whom he is little acquainted, to the detriment of his newly wedded wife and his most intimate friend"— which, if looked at in the light of real life, is absurd. To put the point again, quoting Stoll's words once more, "the generous and unsuspicious hero, believing a person whom he does not love or really know and has no right reason to trust, . . . falls, in the self-same scene, without proof of the accuser's or inquiry and investigation of his own, into a jealous rage, and resolves . . . secretly to kill the person suspected."

It is unlikely, in Stoll's view, that such a man as Othello is made out by Shakespeare to be would in real life believe the wrong person in this way. "No doubt," he writes, "proof of the falseness of the loved one might lead a trustful child or man to be suspicious generally; but into suspicion Othello is precipitated, without proof. And it is only . . . by means of a specious and unreal psychology that he is made incapable of distrusting the testimony which his nature forbids him to accept, to the point of distrusting the testimony and character of those whom both his nature and their own forbid him to discredit. 'His unquestioning faith in Desdemona is his life,' says Sir Walter Raleigh—in so far that he immediately forsakes her and turns wholly to Iago!"

The tragedy of *Othello*, then, according to Professor Stoll, centres in a great improbability. A hero of great nobility of character, unsuspicious, not in the least prone to jealousy, falls an instant victim to the insinuations of a man whom he has far less reason to trust than he has to trust the people against whom the insinuations are made: nevertheless, contrary to all real-life probability, the hero becomes immediately jealous—a man pre-eminently free from jealousy becomes on the instant markedly jealous. And Professor Stoll, emphasizing this central improbability, points out the distinction between real life on the one hand and dramatic art on the other.

A play—at any rate a Shakespeare play—is not necessarily a sequence of events that would be likely to occur in real life: it does not necessarily involve consistent real-life psychology. And much unsound criticism has resulted, Stoll claims, from critics taking fiction for fact. "They turn the impossibilities into possibilities, and the poetry into prose; . . . their ears are caught by the weaker accents, not the stronger." What Shakespeare is concerned with is "not primarily the image of life but an illusion, and, as its consequence, a greater emotional effect than the mere image of life can give." Shakespeare asks of his audience what Coleridge called "that willing suspension of disbelief, for the moment, which constitutes poetic faith."

But many critics have taken his plays—and many still do—
as if they were entirely concerned with trains of events and with
psychological developments in actual life. "The trouble with
Shakespeare criticism," says Stoll, again, "is that it has been
prompted and guided by the spirit of literalism. The play has
been thought to be a psychological document, not primarily
a play, a structure, both interdependent and independent, the
parts mutually, and sufficiently, supporting and explaining
each other; and the characters have been taken for the separable
copies of reality."

What are we to say of Professor Stoll's theory of *Othello*?

There is no doubt that Iago has no sooner begun his
attack on Othello's peace of mind than Othello becomes
discomposed. Iago's attack begins at III, iii, 35. Iago and
Othello have entered and observed Cassio and Desdemona in
conversation. Cassio goes out, and, before Desdemona joins
the newcomers, the following piece of dialogue takes place:

> *Iago.* Ha! I like not that.
> *Othello.*   What does thou say?
> *Iago.* Nothing, my lord: or if—I know not what.
> *Othello.* Was not that Cassio parted from my wife?
> *Iago.* Cassio, my lord! No, sure, I cannot think it,
>   That he would steal away so guilty-like,
>   Seeing you coming.
> *Othello.*   I do believe 'twas he.
>   (III, iii, 35–40)

It seems clear that Othello is already uneasy. Iago has but
just begun his suggestions, and Othello has already fallen a
victim to them. Othello's tone is surely one of unhappiness.
Desdemona comes up, and in a moment she is asking Othello
to call Cassio back: he replies:

> Not now, sweet Desdemona; some other time.
>   (III, iii, 55)

He is disturbed: she is still "sweet Desdemona", but he is
unhappy: the germ of suspicion is already within him. And
as the remainder of the scene proceeds we see Iago continuing
his crafty wiles, and we see Othello in a variety of moods.
He speaks of how he loves Desdemona: he insists that he
must have proof before he will doubt her. But on the other

hand he *does* doubt her, his peace of mind is shattered, and at some points he speaks with terrible passion.

Now it must be allowed that he has not been jealous before this scene, nor is there any suggestion that he has ever been prone to jealousy. During his wooing of Desdemona he was assisted by Cassio who "went between us very oft" (III, iii, 100), and there was apparently no question of jealousy. Do we then have a transition from non-jealousy to jealousy which is improbable in terms of real life? I do not think so. Before the beginning of Iago's temptation of Othello the idea of jealousy had never occurred to Othello spontaneously, for admittedly he is not naturally jealous: nor had it been suggested to him by any disinterested person. It is true that Brabantio had said:

> Look to her, Moor, if thou hast eyes to see:
> She has deceived her father, and may thee.
> (I, iii, 293–4)

But Othello might easily decide to pay no attention to this: after all, Brabantio was disgruntled, to say the least. (His words might of course sink down into Othello's subconscious mind, to reappear in his conscious mind later on at a critical moment.) I would suggest that, in terms of real life, there is nothing improbable about the following. Othello is not himself predisposed to jealousy, and no disinterested person suggests the idea of jealousy to him before III, iii, 35. But at that point Iago begins to suggest the idea to him. Now Iago has a widespread reputation for integrity. Again and again he is called "honest" by people who know him. His reputation for honesty is repeatedly emphasized by Shakespeare. There is therefore good enough reason for Othello to feel inclined to believe Iago; and there are reasons which might well make him feel qualms of doubt concerning Desdemona's fidelity *after* someone apparently disinterested had suggested the conception of jealousy to him.

I have already suggested that those words of Brabantio— "She has deceived her father, and may thee"—not heeded at the time by Othello in his conscious mind, might have sunk into his subconscious mind, the idea to reappear with sinister force in his conscious mind later. And there are other considerations which might well conspire to make him jealous once the keynote had been sounded by "honest" Iago. Othello is a Moor—his skin is black—those with whom he associates are of a different race and colour, and some of them look down on him. The angry Brabantio speaks to Othello of "the sooty bosom of such a thing as thou" (I, ii, 70–1), and later he speaks of Desdemona having fallen "in love with what she fear'd to look on", this being "against all rules of nature" (I, iii, 98, 101). Invoking the facts of real-life psychology, one might well suggest that Othello might have had a deep-rooted inferiority complex on account of his race and colour: he might well himself wonder sometimes how Desdemona could have brought herself to love him: and he might have a subconscious fear that she would easily enough fall out of love with him and transfer her affection to one of her own race. This fear might remain entirely subconscious until the idea of jealousy had been implanted in him by an apparently reputable person.

Again, Othello is distinguished by a sense of humility quite apart from any question of race. He is a soldier: he is not skilled in the arts of peace. "Rude am I in my speech", he says (I, iii, 81), "And little bless'd with the soft phrase of peace." On this ground, too, he may from the beginning feel, deep down within himself, that he has little to offer Desdemona—that she may not find him congenial for very long. And again, he is not a youth: he is middle-aged. At III, iii, 265, he speaks of himself as "declined into the vale of years." Here again he may have a subconscious fear right from the start that Desdemona will tire of him and find that she wants a younger man for her lover. All these considerations rise to the surface of his mind after the temptation has begun:

> Haply, for I am black
> And have not those soft parts of conversation
> That chamberers have, or for I am declined
> Into the vale of years,—yet that's not much—
> She's gone. I am abused; and my relief
> Must be to loathe her.

(III, iii, 263–8)

After the temptation has begun, Iago speaks to Othello of

how "In Venice they do let heaven see the pranks They dare not show their husbands" (III, iii, 202–3)—that is, he exploits the fact that Othello, being of an alien race, may feel that he does not know the habits of the Venetians very well. Further, Iago refers to Desdemona as one who "did deceive her father, marrying you" (III, iii, 206); and he speaks of how unnatural it is for a woman to marry one of an alien race (III, iii, 228 ff.).

Professor Stoll thinks that a noble man like Othello would naturally trust rather the wife who meant so much to him than Iago, a person he had much less reason to trust. But can we be at all sure of this? On the one hand, Iago has a widespread reputation for integrity; on the other hand, there is more than one reason why Othello could suppose that Desdemona might eventually find him uncongenial. Professor Stoll regards it as improbable that Othello, not jealous and not prone to jealousy at the outset, should, on Iago's suggestion, become jealous. I do not regard that as improbable either. Our argument is that before the temptation he is not jealous, certainly; but there are possibilities of suspicion which may well be present in his subconscious mind from the start (without detracting from his essential nobility). When an apparently honourable and disinterested person suggests the idea of jealousy to him, these possibilities of suspicion can emerge into his consciousness to reinforce that idea of jealousy. Iago actually refers to some of them: Othello himself refers to others. I cannot honestly see that, in terms of real life, there is anything improbable about all this. And there is another point that must be made.

The temptation by Iago begins at III, iii, 35. By the end of III, iii, we have already seen Othello shaken by tremendous passion. We have already seen in him a man in whom passion preponderates over reason; and the condition becomes worse and worse as the second half of the play proceeds. At climactic points it becomes a frenzy.

Now what of Othello before the temptation by Iago begins? Does he, before the temptation, impress us as a man who is liable to allow his reason to abdicate in favour of passion? Lodovico, from Venice, having seen Othello striking and insulting Desdemona, having seen him storm out shouting "Goats and monkeys!", says in amazement:

> Is this the noble Moor whom our full senate
> Call all in all sufficient? Is this the nature
> Whom passion could not shake?

(IV, i, 275–7)

These lines describe Othello as Venice knew him, before the temptation. Can such a change be psychologically credible?

But there is evidence in the play that Lodovico and the "full senate" were not altogether correct in their estimate of Othello. Iago was regarded in Venice as a man most conspicuous for honesty. At the very moments when he is plotting his unspeakable villainies Iago is referred to as "honest". That is to say, to his fellow-characters in the play, Iago seems different from what he really is: appearance belies reality. If Venice is totally wrong in its estimate of Iago, must we necessarily suppose that it was totally right in its estimate of Othello? Othello seems to his acquaintance in Venice to be a man whose nature cannot be shaken by passion. He seems to be a man whose reason is never in danger of being overthrown by passion. But he himself, out of his own mouth, gives evidence that this is not quite so. In Act II, scene iii, he enters to investigate the fracas involving Cassio and Montano. And at lines 204 ff. he says this:

> Now, by heaven,
> My blood begins my safer guides to rule;
> And passion, having my best judgment collied,
> Assays to lead the way: if I once stir,
> Or do but lift this arm, the best of you
> Shall sink in my rebuke.

Could anything be more explicit? This is one of those pieces of "self-explanation" by Shakespearian characters which readers of Professor L. L. Scühcking's book *Character Problems in Shakespeare's Plays* (1922) readily recognize as such. There is no reason to suppose that Shakespeare is making Othello say something which is not true. On the contrary, surely Shakespeare is himself guiding us. By his "blood" Othello means passion. The word "collied" means "blackened". Passion, Othello declares, has blackened his reason, and is trying to get control over his personality. This does not actually happen here—Othello controls himself successfully. But the point is this—that here, before any question of distrust of Desdemona has arisen, Othello's own words indicate to us that he is a man in whom, at critical points, passion is liable to try to get the upper hand over reason.

Apparently no one in Venice thinks that he is such a man: it is doubtless a case of a noble man with an evil potentiality which he manages to keep secret, to control, until he comes to suspect Desdemona in III, iii. There, however, after the distrust of Desdemona has been implanted in his mind, when we see him becoming more and more passionate and unreasonable, we remember, and are meant by Shakespeare to remember, that before this matter ever arose we learned that Othello was liable to show this kind of reaction. Surely by this means Shakespeare endeavours to give us the idea of a character psychologically consistent before and after the beginning of the temptation. Professor Stoll deals with the Cassio-Montano affair, but he refuses to allow that it has any psychological significance. He says: "Here Othello, who hitherto, according to our own impression and his friends' report, could never be ruffled, gets angry with Cassio, adopts, despite prepossession in his favour, Iago's false report without investigation, and is, in a way, 'tenderly led by the nose' already. But these preparations are dramatic, poetic, not psychological; they arouse tragic misgivings, rather than rational, logical expectations. And this minor improbability in Othello's conduct as governor only makes more acceptable the similar and greater one as a husband when it comes."

But I cannot agree that there is no psychological factor involved. Othello declares that his passion is trying to get the better of his reason: surely the audience is actually being invited to think that the hero's passion may try to do that again, and may even succeed. And when a man speaks of his "passion" and his "best judgment" he is certainly speaking in psychological terms.

. . . . .

Shakespeare's handling of the hero in this play, then, it

B

seems to me, is quite in accord with real-life psychological probability. But admittedly there is some psychological unrealism in the play. Iago professes a number of motives for his proceeding against Othello and Cassio. Among these motives is the fact that he suspects both of them of having seduced his wife Emilia. "I hate the Moor," he says at I, iii, 392,

> And it is thought abroad, that 'twixt my sheets
> He has done my office: I know not if 't be true;
> But I, for mere suspicion in that kind,
> Will do as if for surety.

Again, at II, i, 304, he says:

> I do suspect the lusty Moor
> Hath leap'd into my seat; the thought whereof
> Doth, like a poisonous mineral, gnaw my inwards;
> And nothing can or shall content my soul
> Till I am even'd with him, wife for wife,
> Or failing so, yet that I put the Moor
> At least into a jealousy so strong
> That judgement cannot cure.

And a line or two later he says:

> I fear Cassio with my night-cap too.

Now from this one must surely get the impression that Iago is a man who exemplifies sexual jealousy very strongly indeed. He suspects of seducing his wife, not just one man, but two. And he declares that the thought of Othello having seduced Emilia "gnaws his inwards" so that he is insatiable for revenge. But once Iago has started his machinations against Othello and Cassio, can we really say that we do in fact feel that he is an abnormal case of sexual jealousy? I do not think so. He does not speak or behave like such a man. There is surely psychological inconsistency here. Again, Iago declares that he himself loves Desdemona:

> I do love her too;
> Not out of absolute lust, though peradventure
> I stand accountant for as great a sin,
> But partly led to diet my revenge, ...
> (II, i, 300–3)

Noting the words "though peradventure . . . a sin" we must

take it that Iago is admitting that he loves Desdemona in a lustful manner. So he says here: but can we say that anywhere in the play he acts as if in fact he did love her? I do not think so.

In Shakespeare's handling of Iago, then, there is a measure of psychological unrealism. Now there is plenty of psychological unrealism elsewhere in Shakespeare also. And unless we recognize it for what it is we shall be in danger of making bad mistakes in interpretation. There are places where we have a character speaking and acting in a way different from the way in which such a character in real life would be likely to speak and act. There are places where, if we insist on judging the character as if it were a matter of real life, we will find ourselves disapproving of him or her, whereas Shakespeare clearly intends the character to be regarded sympathetically all through. In his book, *Shakespearian Comedy and Other Studies*, published posthumously in 1944, George Gordon refers to some cases of this non-realism. He writes so delightfully that I cannot forbear quoting one case *in extenso*:

> Even in so mature and so masterly a play as *Twelfth Night* we are presented, in the hypothesis, with a young lady—the central figure of the play—who puns with sailors on an unknown coast, having just been rescued from the water, and, as she supposed, seen her brother drowned before her eyes. Yet she puns. Nor is this all. With her clothes still dripping from her immersion she hastens to inquire who rules in these parts, and on being told, and hearing that the prince is a bachelor remarks, in effect, that this will do. She decides there and then to supplant the lady whom he courts.

Now, it is no doubt true that any ordinary woman in Viola's position—far from inventing, at such a moment, so ambitious a scheme of life—would have hastened to disclose herself to the nearest consul, and resume her journey. Because presumably she was *going* somewhere; and we know that she was penniless. On this way of thinking, the whole incident becomes monstrous and improbable. Viola is either inhuman or unreal. It is, however, the hypothesis of *Twelfth Night* that Viola does none of the things which an ordinary young woman would have done in her position, but forms instead, and instantly, the bold design which the play unravels. We *can*, of course, refuse this; but do we? It is asking a good deal more of us than most modern

> dramatists do; but something must be allowed to Romance.
> All fiction rests upon belief. Romance lives by it. Belief is its
> whole capital; and what does it matter if now and then the
> account is a little overdrawn? That bank, even to-day, can
> stand it. The dramatist like Shakespeare who goes beyond life
> to please us is entitled to a larger share of our credulity. It is
> our one way of paying him; and there is no price which, I
> believe, we pay so easily, or with half so good a will.[1]

Apply the criteria of judgment that one would apply in real
life, and Viola becomes "inhuman or unreal". But certainly
Shakespeare does not intend us to think of her as being either
of these things.

Another case in point is Rosalind. Mr. S. L. Bethell
refers to this case.[2] "Why," he asks, "does not Rosalind
present herself to her father as soon as she discovers him in
the forest of Arden?

> I met the duke yesterday and had much question with him
> [she says]: he asked me of what parentage I was; I told him, of
> as good as he; so he laughed and let me go.
>
> (*A.Y.L.I.* III, iv, 38)

Must we write her down as heartless and unfilial," Mr. Bethell
asks, "despite her earlier outburst of grief at her father's long
banishment? Shakespeare supplies no motive, but his own
motive is plain enough: Rosalind is required to play Ganymede
for some time longer, and all meetings of long parted relatives
must be left for the dénouement in the Masque of Hymen.
Any psychological explanation of Rosalind's behaviour would
introduce into her character a warring element foreign to the
writer's intention." Judge her failure to reveal her identity to
her father by the criteria one would use in real life, and one
might well conclude her to be "heartless and unfilial". But
certainly Shakespeare does not intend us to take her so at all.

Drama in which the events presented are such as could
happen exactly so in real life, and in which the characters are
to be estimated precisely as such people would be estimated
in real life, is called "naturalistic" drama. We are dealing with
instances of non-naturalism in Shakespeare. Another instance,

[1] Op. cit. pp. 22–23.
[2] *Shakespeare and the Popular Dramatic Tradition* (1944), p. 67.

a famous instance, is to be found in *I Henry IV*, I, ii, 218 ff. This is a soliloquy spoken by Prince Hal, at the end of the first scene in which we have witnessed him in the company of Falstaff. It has been an amusing scene, and it has contained the promise of further amusement. Yet at the end of the scene, left alone, Hal apostrophizes Falstaff and his crew thus:

> I know you all, and will awhile uphold
> The unyoked humour of your idleness:
> Yet herein will I imitate the sun,
> Who doth permit the base contagious clouds
> To smother up his beauty from the world,
> That, when he please again to be himself,
> Being wanted, he may be more wonder'd at,
> By breaking through the foul and ugly mists
> Of vapours that did seem to strangle him.
> If all the year were playing holidays,
> To sport would be as tedious as to work;
> But when they seldom come, they wish'd for come,
> And nothing pleaseth but rare accidents.
> So, when this loose behaviour I throw off
> And pay the debt I never promised,
> By how much better than my word I am,
> By so much shall I falsify men's hopes;
> And like bright metal on a sullen ground,
> My reformation, glittering o'er my fault,
> Shall show more goodly and attract more eyes
> Than that which hath no foil to set it off.
> I'll so offend, to make offence a skill;
> Redeeming time when men think least I will.

Does this soliloquy mean that every time we see the prince in the company of his boon companions we are to say to ourselves "That young man is an egregious hypocrite"? Are we to allow the soliloquy, coming as it does near the beginning of the first part of the long two-part play, to prejudice us against the prince all the way through the work? Are we to say, "He is sowing his wild oats, but he is a hypocrite as well, which is much worse"?

Professor Schücking calls the monologue "very remarkable". He goes on:[1] "If we were to take it literally it would

[1] *Character Problems in Shakespeare's Plays*, p. 219.

stamp the Prince's character with the mark of gross hypocrisy, which was certainly not intended. We are astonished to find Prince Hal maintaining that he mixes in the company of the rascals merely in order to make his own virtues shine all the more splendidly afterward. If that were true he would thereby become, as Kreyssig says, 'a theatrical young wastrel, who makes a great show of sowing his wild oats in order afterward to create a sensation by his conversion'. This, however, is most probably not the fundamental structure of the character.''

The explanation of the soliloquy accepted by most critics is that which Schücking gives in the following words:[1] ''The fact is, this monologue has to be regarded not as an individual expression, imagined as being psychologically consistent with the character of the speaker, and perhaps even as intended to show him as deceiving himself, but as an explanatory remark, meant to be true to fact and belonging to the exposition, a statement which might have been put into the mouth of some one speaking as Chorus.''

The speech may be regarded as having been written in order to protect Hal's character in the audience's estimation. As the audience sees the prince sowing these wild oats of his, it knows that in the end he is going to reform and that men are going to be amazed by the reformation. Thus it is not unduly worried by the sowing of the wild oats. The audience is given a preview of what in the end actually happens. Shakespeare wanted the audience to have that preview, and so at the end of I, ii, he used Hal to fulfil a Chorus-function. Since he was making Hal himself speak prophetically, Shakespeare could hardly in the soliloquy dispense with the idea of motive. But the audience is not supposed to take Hal's professed motive very seriously.

Take this soliloquy naturalistically—take the words as directly bearing on the speaker's present character—and his character is thereby damaged instead of being protected. If we take it so, then Shakespeare's intention in writing the speech will have been completely frustrated. The effect will be the opposite of what he wanted to produce.

Another famous piece of non-naturalistic writing in

[1] *Character Problems in Shakespeare's Plays*, p. 221.

Shakespeare occurs in the opening speech in *Richard III*. The speech is delivered by Richard, Duke of Gloucester, who afterwards becomes King Richard III. He speaks of his physical deformity which prevents him from becoming a lover; he is not "shaped for sportive tricks, Nor made to court an amorous looking-glass" (I, i, 14–15). And he goes on, at line 28, to say this:

> And therefore, since I cannot prove a lover,
> To entertain these fair well-spoken days,
> I am determined to prove a villain
> And hate the idle pleasures of these days.
> Plots have I laid, inductions dangerous,
> By drunken prophecies, libels and dreams,
> To set my brother Clarence and the king
> In deadly hate the one against the other:
> And if King Edward be as true and just
> As I am subtle, false and treacherous,
> This day should Clarence closely be mew'd up . . . .

As Mr. Bethell says,[1] "Gloucester speaks of himself dispassionately, like an onlooker. No one actually 'determines to prove a villain' or estimates himself as 'subtle, false and treacherous'." And again: "Gloucester's 'I am determined to prove a villain' could never be seriously spoken by mortal man." Shakespeare simply wants the audience to be told at the start what sort of man Gloucester is, and what he is planning to do. Gloucester *is* villainous, subtle, false, and treacherous; and Shakespeare tells us this by the simple expedient of making Gloucester tell us it—even though in real life no one would speak of himself as Gloucester does. Psychological probability is set aside for the time being.

Let us have one other example. Towards the end of the first scene of *Hamlet* we have a beautiful couple of lines spoken by Horatio:

> But, look, the morn, in russet mantle clad,
> Walks o'er the dew of yon high eastward hill.

Here, as Professor Dover Wilson notes,[2] "the word 'russet',

[1] *Shakespeare and the Popular Dramatic Tradition*, pp. 71, 73.
[2] *Hamlet*, The New Shakespeare (1936), p. xxxvi.

used to describe the indeterminate reddish-brown or grey of
the sky at daybreak, recalls the coarse homespun cloth, which
is its original sense, and so gives birth to the image of Dawn
as a labourer mounting the hill to his work of the day, his
mantle thrown across his shoulder." It is beautifully poetic
and imaginative. But is it the sort of speech that a man of
Horatio's character (sturdy, full of common sense, even
stolid) would be expected to utter? I hardly think so. But
Shakespeare wants us, after the tenseness of the night-scene,
to have this particular imaginative impression of daybreak—
he wants us to change our mood: and he gets us to do so by
means of these lines—he does not care whether or not the
lines fully accord with the speaker's character. And in interpreting the play as a whole it would be unwise, on the basis
of these lines, to take it that Horatio has the soul of a poet.[1]

.   .   .   .   .

Shakespeare's contemporary audiences were not dis-
concerted by non-naturalism in the drama. We may understand this the more readily if we bear in mind the stage conditions of his day. The following account is extremely sketchy,
but it will serve for our purpose.[2]

The public theatres were quite small buildings, square,
circular, or hexagonal. (We possess the specifications of one
of them, the Fortune, which was square, the exterior measurements being eighty feet by eighty, the interior measurements
fifty-five feet by fifty-five.) Inside, there were three tiers of
galleries running round, surmounted by a roof. The part
of the theatre corresponding to our pit and orchestra stalls
was open to the sky, and here the less wealthy spectators
(the "groundlings") stood, or perhaps sat on stools.

The main part of the stage jutted out into the theatre, so
that if playing to a full house the actors, when on the main
part of the stage, had spectators on three sides of them. Above
the stage there was a balcony, or "upper stage", on which

---

[1] This case is cited by Mr. Bethell, op. cit., p. 72.
[2] Accounts of the Elizabethan public theatre are to be found in various
books. I would mention that in Chapter V of Dr. G. B. Harrison's *Introducing Shakespeare* Pelican Books, 1939), because it gives me the opportunity of recommending this excellent little book to my readers in its entirety.

action could take place when a scene involved some elevated place, e.g. the wall of Harfleur in *Henry V*, Cleopatra's monument, Juliet's balcony, etc. The space under the upper stage—the inner stage—could also be used for action, and would be especially appropriate for an interior setting—a cavern, a bedroom, etc. The inner stage was provided with a curtain: the main part of the stage, protruding into the auditorium, had no curtain. Above the upper stage a canopy jutted out over the whole proscenium, so that the players were protected from rain though the groundlings were not! Entrances and exits were effected by means of two doors at the back of the main part of the stage, one to the right of the inner stage curtain, the other to the left of it. Properties were used on a considerable scale, but there was no stage scenery. And performances took place in daylight.

Even from this all too brief account it will be clearly seen that an Elizabethan or Jacobean performance of a Shakespeare play was in various respects very different from a present-day performance. What we want to stress mainly here is that there is a great deal more verisimilitude in a modern performance than there was in an Elizabethan or Jacobean one. We have our darkened auditorium, our picture stage, our lavish scenery, and our elaborate stage lighting. The art of the stage technicians can virtually present to our eyes a cold, midnight scene at the beginning of *Hamlet*, a stormy scene with fog and filthy air at the beginning of *Macbeth*, a lovely moonlight summer night in the last scene of *The Merchant of Venice*. But in all three cases Shakespeare's contemporary audience was looking at actors on a stage devoid of scenery and illuminated by the broad light of day. The only way that Shakespeare could suggest an eerie, cold, midnight scene— a foggy and filthy atmosphere—a moonlit summer night— was by means of the words he put into the mouths of his characters. And the audience would have to use its imagination. A contemporary Shakespearian audience, witnessing the opening of *Hamlet*, might see around it all the evidences of a fine, bright afternoon: listening to the dialogue, it would involuntarily agree to allow that the action was taking place at midnight in bitterly cold weather.

The fact that Shakespeare's contemporary audiences were thus accustomed to much less verisimilitude than we are nowadays would make them tend to be all the less troubled by lack of realism at a given point as regards plot-sequence or characterization.

Now, of course, it is only sometimes that Shakespeare goes counter to real-life probability in plot-sequence and characterization. Often he does not. This chapter began with an attempt to show that in *Othello* the hero's psychological development is, *pace* Professor Stoll, perfectly consistent with real life. Shakespeare is often "true to life": often he is not. To be able to distinguish between the two elements, the naturalistic and the non-naturalistic or conventional, is to have a claim to some insight into the true nature of Shakespeare's art.

Diametrically opposed to such views as those of Professor Stoll are the views of critics who apply to the interpretation of Shakespeare's plays the principles of psycho-analysis. A psycho-analytic critic will take a character in a Shakespeare play and interpret his words and behaviour just as if the character in question were a real-life patient in the critic's consulting room. The psycho-analytic critic will take a whole play, and, interpreting it, produce an analysis of Shakespeare's own psyche at the period when he wrote it, the critic treating the play in the same way as he would in a consulting-room treat a patient's conversation—the narration of dreams, and so on. And this revelation of Shakespeare's own psyche at the time indicates the true interpretation of the meaning of the play. So it is claimed.

A well-known example of this type of criticism is to be found in a paper by Dr. Ernest Jones, entitled *The Oedipus-Complex as an Explanation of Hamlet's Mystery: A Study in Motive*.[1] In this essay Dr. Jones develops a theory of *Hamlet* first advanced by Sigmund Freud. Dr. Jones's essay is most

---

[1] *The American Journal of Psychology*, Vol. XXI (1910), pp. 72 ff. All my quotations from Dr. Jones are from this article. In 1949 Dr. Jones published a book entitled *Hamlet and Oedipus*. My manuscript was completed before I saw this book.

interesting, and he argues very skilfully and persuasively: but
it seems to me that there are certain things to be said against
this sort of interpretation of literary works.

Dr. Jones's paper is of considerable length, and we have
space here to indicate his theory of *Hamlet* only in the most
summary fashion. According to him, we have, in the hero
of this play, a man who finds himself unable to fulfil a certain
duty, to perform a certain action, on account of a subconscious
mental conflict which is a renewal of a conflict he had
experienced in his childhood. Hamlet, according to this
view, never doubts that it is his duty to kill Claudius, but he
has a deep-seated reluctance to do so, and he puts off the deed
by means of various specious excuses. He does not himself
understand why he does so, because the reason lies in his
subconscious mind.

In his childhood, according to Freud and Jones, Hamlet
exemplified the well-known "Oedipus-complex", that is,
he had loved his mother in an erotic sense and hated his
father as being his rival for his mother's affection. He had
had a desire to take his father's place in the affection of his
mother. This desire had been "repressed", and love and
respect for his father had supervened. All this is perfectly
in accord with what psycho-analysts find to be common
enough in real life.

At the beginning of the play we find Hamlet in a morbid
mental condition on account of the second marriage of his
mother. What has happened is that the hero's uncle, Claudius,
has supplanted the hero's father, the elder Hamlet, in the
affections of the hero's mother, Gertrude—which is what,
in his childhood, the hero himself had wanted to do. The
sight of Claudius doing this stirs up in Hamlet's subconscious
mind the old desire which had been repressed, and it is the
renewal of this subconscious trouble that causes Hamlet to
fall into the morbid state in which we find him at the outset.
To quote Dr. Jones's words: "Now comes the father's death
and the mother's second marriage. The long 'repressed' desire
to take his father's place in his mother's affection is stimulated
to unconscious activity by the sight of someone usurping
this place exactly as he himself had once longed to do. More,

this someone was a member of the same family, so that the actual usurpation further resembled the imaginary one in being incestuous. Without his being at all aware of it these ancient desires are ringing in his mind, are once more struggling to find expression, and need such an expenditure of energy again to 'repress' them that he is reduced to the deplorable mental state he himself so vividly depicts."

Then Hamlet is informed by the Ghost that Claudius is a murderer. He becomes aware that his uncle had murdered his father and, as one result, thus been able to marry the mother. The child in the grip of the Oedipus-complex desires the death of the rival-father—desires moreover himself to kill the father—so that he may enjoy the mother with no competition. "Hamlet's second guilty wish," says Dr. Jones, "had thus also been realized by his uncle, namely to procure the fulfilment of the first—the replacement of his father—by a personal deed, in fact by murder."

Hamlet has, laid upon him by the Ghost, the duty of exacting vengeance from Claudius. Hamlet, according to this theory, never questions that it *is* his duty to do this, but he finds himself unable to proceed effectively—he has a deep-rooted aversion to the deed, for some reason which he does not know. The reason, according to Dr. Jones's theory, is this: the old Oedipus-complex has been re-awakened in Hamlet's subconscious mind, and Hamlet is, in his sub-conscious mind, in the process of repressing it again. That is, he is in the process of repressing a desire to murder his mother's husband. Claudius is his mother's husband (the fact that he is her second husband is not relevant here); and so Hamlet is in his subconscious mind repressing the wish to do what he consciously realizes it is his duty to do. This is the reason, unknown to him himself, why he is so reluctant to kill Claudius. As Dr. Jones puts it, "The call of duty to slay his uncle cannot be obeyed because it links itself with the call of his nature to slay his mother's husband, whether this is the first or the second; the latter call is strongly 'repressed', and therefore necessarily the former also."

Now, of course, Shakespeare cannot have been aware of any of this—that will be readily granted. But what Dr. Jones contends is that Shakespeare, when he wrote *Hamlet*, was himself, in his own subconscious mind, in Hamlet's condition. Hamlet, then, is in this respect an unconscious portrait of Shakespeare himself. This idea has been advanced by various critics whose interpretations of the play are not psycho-analytic. Dr. Jones is able to say that "the view that Shakespeare depicted in Hamlet his own inner self is a wide-spread one."

In a passage in his book *The English Poetic Mind* (1932), that distinguished critic, Mr. Charles Williams, speaks of the possibility that when he wrote *Hamlet* "Shakespeare was not then capable of making Hamlet act, that the development of his genius had reached precisely the point where it was intensely aware of man's distracted mind, of its own divided mind, and was not able to solve the problem. In short, that it is Shakespeare, and not Hamlet, who is seeking the springs of action, and he rather than the prince who therefore here delays;" and again—"Hamlet is, after all, a figure in a play. To say that he cannot discover within himself the initiative of action is to say that Shakespeare could not or would not discover it for him. Is it too much to say that Shakespeare would not because he could not? that he made *Hamlet* because he himself was trying to reach by his genius a poetic comprehension of the place where men act?"[1] Mr. Williams by no means interprets the play as Dr. Jones does: he does not psycho-analyze systematically. But Mr. Williams too is prepared to see in Hamlet a projection of Shakespeare himself, as indeed many critics in their different ways are.

What are we to say about Freud's and Jones's inter-pretation of *Hamlet*? I have already expressed appreciation of Dr. Jones's skill and persuasiveness in argument. And there are things in his essay with which one readily agrees. But as to his main thesis, sketched out above, I feel that there are dangers involved. And I feel that these dangers are inherent in all psycho-analytic interpretation of literature. One readily admits that the condition of the author's subconscious mind has a vital bearing on the finished work of art. Of course it has. But there is another factor too—the author's conscious

[1] Op. cit., pp. 66, 68.

shaping power. Shakespeare certainly had his consciou
intentions as he wrote *Hamlet*. Scholarship can say, wit
varying degrees of confidence at various points, what thes
were. Dr. Jones brushes these conscious intentions aside a
irrelevant to the true interpretation of the play.

"It is here maintained," he says in his essay, "that thi
conflict is an echo of a similar one in Shakspeare himself
as to a greater or less extent it is in all men. It is, therefore
as much beside the point to enquire into Shakspeare'
conscious intention, moral or otherwise, in the play as it i
in the case of most works of genius. The play is the form in
which his feeling finds its spontaneous expression, withou
any inquiry being possible on his part as to the essential natur
or source of that feeling." Now this view of literature is on
which, as I say, makes me uncomfortable. The question is
what is the essential *Hamlet*? If scholarship can show that th
play embodies a certain pattern clearly intended by the author
and if this pattern differs significantly from the pattern foun
in it by psycho-analysis, I should say that (admitting tha
both patterns may be said to exist, and may even coincide a
some points) the former constitutes the essential *Hamlet*

Shakespeare inherits certain material from his literar
source or sources; this passes into his subconscious min
and is there transmuted; it then rises into his conscious min
and is there further transmuted—modified by his consciou
shaping power. The essential *Hamlet* is, to me, what emerge
from all this. The intentions of which Shakespeare was con
scious are, to me, very important indeed. And I should b
bold enough to claim that, as regards his conscious shapin
power, Shakespeare might deliberately go counter to thos
subconscious impulses to which the psychiatrists point, an
of which he himself cannot at all have been aware. Surely on
can, with one's intelligence, construct a design that differ
from what one's design would be if one's subconscious min
had complete control to the exclusion of one's conscious.
must profess myself to be interested in the final product
and the nature of that final product has been at least partl
conditioned by the author's conscious intentions.

Thinking as he does regarding Shakespeare's intentions

Dr. Jones would not be much impressed by any attempt to show that his interpretation was in fact at variance with these intentions. To those, however, who sympathize with what I have been trying to say, it may be of interest to note that at certain points it is. Let me quote him again: "Highly significant is the fact that the grounds Hamlet gives for his hesitancy are grounds none of which will stand a moment's serious consideration, and which continually change from one time to another. One moment he pretends he is too cowardly to perform the deed or that his reason is paralyzed by 'bestial oblivion', at another he questions the truthfulness of the ghost, in another, when the opportunity presents itself in its naked form, he thinks the time is unsuited,—it would be better to wait till the king was in some evil act and then to kill him, and so on. When a man gives at different times a different reason for his conduct it is safe to infer that, whether purposely or not, he is concealing the true reason." Let us concentrate on Hamlet's questioning of the truthfulness of the ghost, and on his conduct in the prayer scene. Does Shakespeare want us to think as Dr. Jones thinks?

Consider the very last speech in Act II, scene ii—Hamlet's soliloquy beginning "O, what a rogue and peasant slave am I!" He has just heard one of the members of the strolling troupe of actors reciting a speech concerning the fall of Troy. This actor has spoken with the utmost feeling—"Tears in his eyes, distraction in 's aspect, A broken voice, . . ." Hamlet contrasts this man with himself:

> What would he do,
> Had he the motive and the cue for passion
> That I have? He would drown the stage with tears . . . .

Hamlet goes on to reproach himself for not having been active about obtaining revenge from Claudius: he must be "pigeon-liver'd"; otherwise he would before this have slain the criminal. He execrates Claudius:

> Remorseless, treacherous, lecherous, kindless villain!
> O, vengeance!

Then he pauses, and reproves himself for falling a-cursing "like a very drab". He must get to business—he must not shout reproaches against himself. And he forms this plan:

> I'll have these players
> Play something like the murder of my father
> Before mine uncle: I'll observe his looks;
> I'll tent him to the quick: if he but blench,
> I know my course.

And he goes on to say:

> The spirit that I have seen
> May be the devil: and the devil hath power
> To assume a pleasing shape; yea, and perhaps
> Out of my weakness and my melancholy,
> As he is very potent with such spirits,
> Abuses me to damn me: I'll have grounds
> More relative than this: the play's the thing
> Wherein I'll catch the conscience of the king.

He has at last been stung to action. But the action he proposes is not the killing of Claudius: it is the verification of the ghost's story. Now the reader may suggest (plenty of critics apart from Dr. Jones have suggested) that here Hamlet is still avoiding his real task. Roused to action he resolves to do something, but it is not what he ought to be doing. It may be suggested (it has been, frequently enough) that it is by specious reasoning that he persuades himself that he must test the ghost's honesty.

I should say that this was quite wrong. In his fascinating book, *What Happens in "Hamlet"* (1935), Professor Dover Wilson has discussed at some length, and very interestingly, the various Elizabethan beliefs that were current concerning the nature of ghosts. According to one view, the ghost which Hamlet had spoken to might very well have been an evil spirit, intent on inducing him to do an evil deed which would bring his soul to damnation. An Elizabethan audience would applaud Hamlet's decision to test the veracity of the ghost. An Elizabethan audience might well say, "This is what he should have done right away: he is now at last doing it: good!" It is true that during and immediately after the ghost's recital Hamlet apparently accepts him as being what he claims to be— his father's spirit. But we may perfectly well suppose that Hamlet would be aware of alternative possibilities regarding ghosts, and it would be perfectly reasonable for him subsequently to form a doubt of which he had not been aware at the time—was it after all in fact my father's spirit, or was it a devil? Indeed, since the latter was a distinct possibility according to Elizabethan belief, it might be said to be Hamlet's positive duty to face the question.

It can be argued—I think rightly—that Hamlet's proper task was this: as soon as he had recovered from the shock caused by the appearance and recital of the ghost, he should have gone about the task of trying to verify its authenticity. It would have been foolish for him to proceed immediately to try to kill Claudius. Actually, he apparently does nothing. At last, at the end of Act II, he resolves to do something—and what he resolves to do is the right thing. No one in possession of the requisite knowledge about Elizabethan conceptions of ghosts can hold that in arranging the play-scene Hamlet is taking refuge behind a quite unnecessary preliminary action. The play-scene is arranged and duly takes place. Claudius gives clear evidence of his guilt. It is now for the first time possible to say that it is Hamlet's duty to proceed directly to kill him. What happens?

At the end of the play-scene Hamlet's mother sends for him. We can hardly reproach him for obeying her summons. He is bound to act in a filial manner. We cannot say that in going to her he is unwarrantably delaying action against Claudius.

But it happens, by force of circumstance, by Fate if we like, that on his way to his mother's room he comes upon Claudius who is on his knees and helpless. Here is Hamlet's opportunity. He has just proved that the ghost was honest: he has just said that he could

> drink hot blood,
> And do such bitter business as the day
> Would quake to look on.

> (III, ii, 408–10)

But he does not kill Claudius. Claudius, he argues, is at prayer: if he dies now, his soul will go to heaven: and what sort of revenge would it be to send the enemy's soul to heaven? Critics have frequently expressed horror at the cruelty of Hamlet's expressed sentiments here. Such inhumanity, they

c

feel, is at variance with the general refinement, sensitivity, and lovableness of Hamlet's spirit. And so, some have said, the reason Hamlet gives for not killing Claudius here cannot be the true reason that is operating in his heart—it must be an excuse. For deep-seated psychological reasons Hamlet is averse to the deed: even now, immediately after the play-scene, he cannot do it; and this is the excuse he gives to himself, an excuse that is unworthy of him.

Now, for my part, I cannot read the scene in this way. It must be remembered that while Shakespeare's Hamlet is, indeed, in general refined, sensitive, and lovable, Shakespeare is writing a play in the sixteenth-century Senecan revenge tragedy tradition. We have good reason to believe that his *Hamlet* is a re-working of an older play, now lost, a pre-Shakespearian *Hamlet*, probably by Thomas Kyd, a play like *The Spanish Tragedy*, definitely in the Senecan tradition. Though the earlier play is lost, we can say with confidence that its hero would not be so refined, sensitive, and lovable as Shakespeare's hero. Shakespeare has subtilized the character in re-working the play. But he has left in the character some elements of the older, more traditional, revenge hero—a ruthlessness, indeed a downright cruelty, which comes out in Shakespeare's hero at more than one point, and which we cannot get around. Let us think, for example, of how he treats Rosencrantz and Guildenstern in the end—they were simply poor tools of the villain and hardly deserved such a fate.

It may be illuminating to compare the case of the ghost. The typical ghost of Senecan revenge tragedy was a crude being from Tartarus. Shakespeare alters the conception. His ghost has dignity, and comes from Purgatory. Shakespeare christianizes his ghost. But still it demands blood-revenge. Would we expect a soul in Purgatory, being purified for ultimate eternal bliss, to be preoccupied with the desire for blood-revenge? Surely not. There is thus a measure of inconsistency here. The ghost is christianized, certainly: but, incongruously, he retains this aspect of the old traditional crude pagan figure.[1]

---

[1] I owe this point to an interesting book, *Hamlet Without Tears* (1946), by I. J. Semper.

I should say it was the same with the hero himself. He is a refinement of a traditional type; but, incongruously, he retains traces of the old type: and his cruelty in the prayer scene is a case in point. Hamlet, in my opinion, is expressing himself perfectly accurately in the prayer scene. He wants vengeance: if he kills Claudius now, Claudius will go to heaven: that is not the sort of vengeance that Hamlet wants: in the revenge drama tradition it would not be revenge at all. And so Hamlet here *must not* kill Claudius.

It is indeed a powerful piece of dramatic irony. Up to the time when he heard the strolling player declaiming the Pyrrhus speech, Hamlet had delayed unwarrantably. Now at last he is spurred to action. He does what he should have done right away—he verifies the ghost's story. Then he is bound to kill Claudius. He is ready to do so. The opportunity presents itself. Fate seems kind. But Fate has really stepped in against Hamlet, for the opportunity presents itself in such a way that it is emphatically Hamlet's duty at this point *not* to kill Claudius. And there is a double irony, for, as we learn at the end of the scene, Claudius's thoughts had remained below: his prayer was not efficacious—it was not really prayer at all: had Hamlet killed him his soul would not have gone to heaven, and vengeance would, in fact, have been secured: but of course Hamlet could not know that.

Not every one will agree with this reading, perhaps. I think it is the reading that Shakespeare intended. Even if the psychiatric critic admitted this, however, as he might, he would—as we have seen—say that it was irrelevant to a true interpretation of the play. It seems to me that the question is just this—what is the play? And my view is that the play is essentially that which the author wanted to communicate to his audiences. I should be prepared to agree that there may be two patterns in *Hamlet*—that which Dr. Jones sees, and that which Shakespeare saw. My real quarrel with Dr. Jones is in connection with the question, which is the more important? To me, Shakespeare's is the more important.

Now, I would point out that I am not saying that psycho-analytic formulae may not be used in a true interpretation of a Shakespeare play—in a true interpretation of the author's intentions. Hamlet is clearly what is called a manic-depressive type—characterized by alternations of elation and depression. But, while Shakespeare could not of course have used such a term, we can say that having observed his fellow-men he knew that there was such a type—that it behaved in such a way: so that to say that Hamlet is a manic-depressive is actually to interpret Shakespeare's conscious intentions accurately.

I would, finally, admit that in a given passage the literary critic may find a tissue of significances which may perhaps not have been present in its totality in Shakespeare's conscious mind as he wrote. But in such cases as I have in mind these significances accord with the over-all design which was in Shakespeare's conscious mind as he wrote the play, and a full appreciation of them enriches our comprehension of his conscious design. This is a very different thing from finding that the entire pattern of a play is totally distinct from anything of which the author can have been aware.

.   .   .   .

In the course of this chapter we have briefly analysed a portion of *Hamlet*. In the process of so doing we noted that, in *Hamlet*, Shakespeare was in all probability re-working an older play, now lost. The older play was doubtless based on sources which are extant—the *Hamlet* story as told in Belleforest's *Histoires Tragiques*, *V* (1576) and/or as told in Saxo Grammaticus's *Historiae Danicae* (twelfth century: printed in 1514). Perhaps Shakespeare consulted one or other or both of these himself as well. At any rate, comparing them with Shakespeare's play, we can say that in *Hamlet* Shakespeare gives us a subtilized re-working of what is essentially a barbaric old story. Shakespeare refines it—but on occasion he retains the barbaric atmosphere, so that we have inconsistency.

We have a similar state of affairs in some other plays. It is important to bear in mind Shakespeare's frequent practice of taking an old story—perhaps in a given case a story which must really be described as a fairy story—and breathing credible life into it. Sometimes, however, it is a case of breathing credible life into *parts* of it and retaining in other parts the fairy-tale atmosphere. Take for example *The Merchant of Venice.* A great deal of the plot material of this play is derived by Shakespeare, directly or indirectly, from a story in an Italian set of tales called *Il Pecorone* by a writer called Ser Giovanni. Here we find among other things the plot-element of the money-lending Jew and the bargain concerning the pound of flesh. Now in the *Il Pecorone* story the Jew is a conventional figure. Shakespeare vitalizes the character. As Sir Arthur Quiller-Couch says, Shakespeare makes Shylock "an intelligible if not a pardonable man; a genuine man, at any rate, of like passions with ourselves . . . makes him entirely more human than the conventional Jew of *Il Pecorone.*"[1] Now in the play which gives us this intensely lifelike figure Shakespeare uses, as another plot-element, the story of the three caskets, which does not come from *Il Pecorone.* The three caskets story is an old legendary motif, which, as again Sir Arthur Quiller-Couch points out, could easily have been borrowed "from the *Gesta Romanorum,* or indeed from any-where."[2] Now in the Shakespeare play this old fairy-tale motif is *not* endowed with life in the way that Shylock is. As we watch the three caskets episode we are well aware that we are in the realm of fairy story.

Furthermore, Shakespeare's characterization of Bassanio conflicts with this very casket story itself, for as he is portrayed in the play Bassanio is not the sort of person who would be likely to choose the leaden casket. As Quiller-Couch says, "I suppose that, while character weighs in drama, if one thing be more certain than another it is that a predatory young gentleman such as Bassanio would *not* have chosen the leaden casket. Let us consider his soliloquy while choosing:

> The world is still deceived with ornament.
> In law, what plea so tainted and corrupt,
> But, being seasoned with a gracious voice,
> Obscures the show of evil? In religion,
> What damnéd error, but some sober brow
> Will bless it, and approve it with a text.

One feels moved to interrupt: 'Yes, yes—and what about

[1] *The New Shakespeare,* "The Merchant of Venice" (1926), p. xviii.
[2] Op. cit., p. x.

yourself, my little fellow? What has altered you, that you, of all men, suddenly use this sanctimonious talk?'"[1] In this play, then, as in various others, we have "truth to life" at some points and at other points the improbability of fairy-tale. The truth to life may be in places so vivid that we may feel tempted to apply true to life criteria to the whole, and thus get into difficulties gratuitously. Because Othello is such an accurate psychological study, we may feel that Iago must be true to life also: but he is not—at any rate not in all respects.

· · · · ·

In our dealings with *Hamlet* it will have been observed that the interpretation of the portion of the play we considered depends on a knowledge of certain aspects of the background of the play—for example, on a knowledge of Elizabethan views concerning the nature of ghosts. I propose now to go on and deal with what is probably the most vitally important piece of background study with which the serious student of Shakespeare's intentions has to cope—a conception of the nature and structure of the universe which underlies every play that Shakespeare wrote.

[1] *The New Shakespeare*, "The Merchant of Venice" (1926), pp. xxv–xxvi.

CHAPTER II

SHAKESPEARE AND THE ORDER-DISORDER ANTITHESIS

SHAKESPEARE was a practical man of the theatre. We cannot doubt that he wrote his plays in order to entertain his audiences, and thus in order that the company of actors for which he wrote, and of which he was a prominent member, should prosper materially. This does not mean that he was not also an artist—of course he was that, quintessentially. He wanted to arouse feelings of aesthetic pleasure in his audiences: and we cannot doubt that as he worked he experienced the satisfaction that the artist feels when he expresses himself, and communicates the results of his mental and emotional experience, in artistic form—and experienced also, perhaps, the feelings of frustration that other artists also experience when they realize that they have not quite succeeded in doing exactly what they set out to do.

Practical man of the theatre, and artist *par excellence*, Shakespeare was a *thinker* too. In a sense he was a learned man. His learning was not that of a don. But his mind was obviously full of philosophical ideas, ideas that we know were floating about among the intelligent and educated of his time, and which he had absorbed. And in his plays he keeps writing with reference to these ideas. It is not Shakespeare's primary purpose to inculcate these ideas—he is not a writer of philosophical text-books. Nor is he a philosophical writer in the sense that Lucretius is, or Dante. Lucretius and Dante are both poets primarily—they are not primarily philosophers. But the *De Rerum Natura* embodies, poetically apprehended, the metaphysic of Epicurus, and the *Divine Comedy* embodies, poetically apprehended, the metaphysic of St. Thomas.

Lucretius's poetic imagination was directly inspired by the Epicurean atomic philosophy, and in his great poem he conveys that philosophy, "passionately apprehended and imaginatively expounded."[1] Dante's poetic imagination was directly inspired by the theology of the schoolmen "as elaborated in the cate-chetical disquisitions of St. Thomas,"[2] and in the *Divine Comedy* he conveys that, again "passionately apprehended and imaginatively expounded." It cannot be said that Shake-speare was primarily inspired by a philosophic system, or that his works are primarily a poetic embodiment of a philo-sophic system. But everything he writes *implies* a philosophy, a "world-picture", which is always present as a background to his work, even if he seldom explicitly states his doctrines. Mr. Eliot speaks of Dante as making "great poetry out of a great philosophy of life," and of Shakespeare as making "equally great poetry out of an inferior and muddled philo-sophy of life." He speaks of Dante's pattern being "the richer by a serious philosophy, and Shakespeare's the poorer by a rag-bag philosophy."[3] I cannot myself agree that Shakespeare's philosophy is a rag-bag one, or muddled. It is certainly true that Shakespeare does not explicitly give us a full statement of his philosophy. But I cannot think that it is muddled. Behind every play that he wrote there lies a picture of the universe and of how it is held together, its separate parts constituting a coherent entity. It is a picture which was visualized not by Shakespeare alone, but also by very many people of his time. An understanding of this picture is necessary to an understanding of the Shakespeare plays.

The picture is a picture of a hierarchically arranged universe in which every created thing has its duly appointed place. The universe, according to this picture, shows *order*. We may for convenience refer to the conception as an order-picture. If any created thing forcibly occupies the position of another created thing, higher or lower in the scale, then we have

---

[1] H. J. C. Grierson, *Metaphysical Lyrics and Poems of the Seventeenth Century: Donne to Butler* (1921), p. xiv.

[2] Ibid., p. xiii.

[3] See Mr. Eliot's introduction to G. Wilson Knight's *The Wheel of Fire*, ed. 1937, pp. xiii, xvii.

disorder. In all his plays Shakespeare is concerned with these conceptions of order and disorder.

To point out the importance of this order-background is now actually a critical commonplace. But it has not been so for very long. In 1936 Professor Lovejoy produced a book entitled *The Great Chain of Being*. Other scholars have followed him, notable among them being Dr. E. M. W. Tillyard and Professor Theodore Spencer. Dr. Tillyard is right in pointing out that "the doctrine of the chain of being was ignored by readers of Elizabethan literature till Lovejoy wrote his book on it; now, our eyes being open, we find it all over the place."[1] Especially useful to students is Dr. Tillyard's own book entitled *The Elizabethan World Picture*; and important also is Professor Spencer's *Shakespeare and the Nature of Man*: both were published in 1943. In the extremely brief and sketchy account of "the Elizabethan world picture" which follows I am simply summarizing material derived from these valuable books.

As Dr. Tillyard points out, in Shakespeare's day the universe was commonly thought of in three ways—as a chain, as a set of parallel planes, and as a dance to music. In connection with the third of these conceptions we may note that Mr. Wilson Knight has shown how often in his imagery Shakespeare thinks of order in terms of harmonious music and of disorder as music out of tune.[2] Let us consider the other two conceptions.

According to the conception of "the great chain of being" we have, under God, in descending sequence, the categories of angelic beings, men, animals, plants, minerals. Angels are superior to men, men are superior to animals, animals to plants, plants to minerals. Minerals have being only: plants have something that minerals do not have—a vegetative soul— they *grow*: animals have being, and the power of growth, and also something else—a sensitive soul—they can see and feel, smell and taste and hear: men can do all that plants and animals can do, they grow, they sense, but in addition they have reason, which the animals do not have—man's reason marks

[1] See Dr. Tillyard's *Shakespeare's History Plays* (1944), p. 18.
[2] See Mr. Wilson Knight's book *The Shakespearian Tempest* (1932).

him off clearly from the animals: angels, above men, are pure
intelligence.

This is a scale of categories. In each of these categories
there are gradations also—among the minerals, for example,
gold is higher in the scale than silver; among the plants the oak
is higher in the scale than the elm; among men a king is higher
than his subjects; among the angelic beings archangels are
higher than ordinary angels; and so on. The whole of reality
is a great hierarchy, a system of degrees, gradations: everything has its duly appointed place in it. Man, it will be
observed, occupies a position between the angels and the beasts.
His reason allies him to the angels: but, if he lets his reason go,
then he becomes like a beast. The reader may remember two
passages from *Hamlet*:

> What a piece of work is a man, how noble in reason, how infinite
> in faculties, in form and moving, how express and admirable
> in action, how like an angel in apprehension, how like a god:
> the beauty of the world; the paragon of animals; . . . .[1]
>
> (II, ii, 316 ff.)

> What is a man,
> If his chief good and market of his time
> Be but to sleep and feed? a beast, no more.
> Sure, he that made us with such large discourse,
> Looking before and after, gave us not
> That capability and god-like reason
> To fust in us unused.
>
> (IV, iv, 33–39)

It is the duty of every created thing to maintain itself in
its own duly appointed place in the hierarchy: it is a sin to
aspire to occupy by force a higher position in the scale than
one is entitled to, and it is equally a sin to occupy a lower
position in the scale than one is entitled to. There is room in
the scheme for *evolution* upwards: but forcible usurpation of a
place in the scale other than one's own is a sin against the law
of order, or "degree' as Shakespeare calls it in *Troilus and
Cressida*. We may speak of the law of order, or the law of
degree: we may equally well speak of the law of nature, for,

---

[1] The text quoted here is that found in Professor Dover Wilson's edition
of the play, where the passage is II, ii, 307-11.

ccording to this conception of reality, order is natural, disrder unnatural. A subject who rebels against his king is roducing disorder: he is also acting unnaturally.

It will be observed that an essential feature of this system s *relation*. Every created thing (apart from the very lowest) oth rules something else and is ruled by something else. The stability of the universe depends on all created things naintaining their relationships with all other created things. There is nothing under God which can be regarded as isolated, elf-sufficient—nothing which is entitled to make its own law or itself.

It should be noted that the order-picture was pre-Copernican and visualized the Ptolemaic planetary system in which he earth stood static at the centre, surrounded by concentric pheres which revolved, carrying round with them the various eavenly bodies. This is the universe as Shakespeare pictured it.

.   .   .   .   .

We have said that, secondly, the Elizabethans thought of eality as a set of parallel planes. Thus we have the plane of he angels, the plane of human society, the plane of the nimals, the plane of the plants, and so on. On each plane we ave a *corresponding* hierarchy. Thus, for example, in the planetary universe the sun is the most resplendent of the eavenly bodies: of flowers, the rose is the finest: in human ociety in a nation the king is the supreme figure. Thus the king *corresponds* to the sun, and *corresponds* to a rose. In *Richard II*, Bolingbroke says that Richard, the king, appears

> As doth the blushing discontented sun
> From out the fiery portal of the east,
> When he perceives the envious clouds are bent
> To dim his glory and to stain the track
> Of his bright passage to the occident.
>
> (III, iii, 63-7)

And in *I Henry IV* Hotspur speaks of Richard as "that sweet ovely rose" (I, iii, 175).

Now, according to the view which Shakespeare shared, f disorder were produced on one plane of reality, a corre-

sponding disorder might well appear on another or on others.
Thus an act producing disorder on one plane might in the last
resort entail a disintegration of the entire universe. Shakespeare's plays are full of instances involving this doctrine of
correspondences. Take for example *Macbeth*. Macbeth kills
his king: by this deed of evil he steps into a higher rank
in human society than he is entitled to: it is a sin against
order, against degree, against nature. Now on the night of
the murder the physical elements are disordered; as Lennox
says:

> The night has been unruly: where we lay,
> Our chimneys were blown down; etc.
>
> (II, iii, 59–60)

" 'Twas a rough night," says Macbeth (and the words have
an ironical significance—it was a rough night for him
spiritually). In II, iv, we have a conversation between Ross
and an Old Man. Ross declares that

> by the clock, 'tis day,
> And yet dark night strangles the travelling lamp,
> (II, iv, 6–7)

i.e. the sun. According to the laws of nature it should be
daylight: actually it is dark: this is a disorder corresponding
to the disorder that Macbeth has unleashed on the plane of
human society. A subject has killed a king in order to take
over his position (inversion): correspondingly, it is dark when
it ought to be light (also inversion). The sun corresponds to
the king: the idea of the sun being strangled by illegitimate
darkness corresponds to the idea of a king being murdered by
a subject. Again, the Old Man tells Ross that

> On Tuesday last,
> A falcon, towering in her pride of place,
> Was by a mousing owl hawk'd at and kill'd.
> (II, iv, 11–13)

According to the laws of nature falcons kill owls: here we have
an inversion of that—a state of disorder in the animal world,
among the birds. The subject-owl kills the exalted falcon,

this again corresponding exactly to Macbeth's deed. Ross
continues:

> And Duncan's horses—a thing most strange and certain—
> Beauteous and swift, the minions of their race,
> Turn'd wild in nature, broke their stalls, flung out,
> Contending 'gainst obedience, as they would make
> War with mankind.
>
> (II, iv, 14–18)

According to the laws of nature, or order, horses obey men:
here we have disorder amongst them, again corresponding to
the disorder in human society caused by Macbeth's deed.
The Old Man corroborates Ross's tale of the horses and
supplies the horrible climax to it:

> 'Tis said they ate each other.
>
> (II, iv, 18)

And Ross:

> They did so, to the amazement of mine eyes
> That look'd upon 't.
>
> (II, iv, 19–20)

We are reminded of the great "degree" speech in *Troilus and
Cressida* in which Ulysses gives what is the fullest and most
explicit statement of the order-doctrine in Shakespeare.
Ulysses describes the terrible effects of disrupting order; and
the ghastly climax is that

> appetite, an universal wolf, ...
> Must make perforce an universal prey,
> And last eat up himself.
>
> (I, iii, 121–4)

This scene in *Macbeth*, then, admirably illustrates the doctrine
of correspondences. Disorder on one plane may be accompanied by disorder on another or others. If the matter is
serious enough, the stability of the whole universe may be
affected. Order, in Shakespeare's philosophy, should be
preserved at all costs. The consequences of disorder anywhere
in the universe may be widespread and dreadful.

* * * * *

Now Shakespeare lived at a time when this conception of

the universe with which we have been dealing was bein
attacked from certain quarters. Consider the following passag
from John Donne. It is taken from his poem *An Anatomy o
the World. The First Anniversary*, written in 1611. He say

> And new philosophy calls all in doubt,
> The element of fire is quite put out;
> The sun is lost, and th' earth, and no man's wit
> Can well direct him where to look for it.
> And freely men confess that this world's spent,
> When in the planets and the firmament
> They seek so many new; they see that this
> Is crumbled out again to his atomies.
> 'Tis all in pieces, all coherence gone,
> All just supply, and all relation:
> Prince, subject, father, son, are things forgot,
> For every man alone thinks he hath got
> To be a phoenix, and that then can be
> None of that kind of which he is but he.
>
> (lines 205–18)

Donne here speaks feelingly of the disintegrational effects o
the New Learning of the Renascence. "New philosophy call
all in doubt." He speaks of the new astronomy, the astronom
of Copernicus. Copernicus opposed the old geocentric uni
versal theory that had held sway in men's minds for so man
centuries. His picture was not the old picture of a static eart
at the centre of the universe. And so, says Donne, "the sun i
lost, and th' earth"—i.e. they are no longer universall
admitted to occupy the places in the scheme of things tha
they had formerly been held to occupy. The effect that Donn
emphasizes is confusion—"no man's wit can well direct hir
where to look for it," where to look for the sun, where t
look for the earth, in the universal scheme. "The element o
fire is quite put out." According to the old theory the eart
was surrounded by the various celestial spheres. The planetar
sphere nearest the earth was that of the moon: but betwee
the earth and the sphere of the moon were the elementa
spheres of water, air, and fire—that of fire being next to th
sphere of the moon. The new Copernican theory, Donne says
has destroyed this conception—"the element of fire is quit

it out." The old universe is gone, and Donne speaks of men's minds as being left in confusion, *déracinés*.

But it is not only in the realm of the physical universe that the old order is gone. "Prince, subject, father, son, are things forgot." According to the old hierarchical conception, the subject was below the prince, the son below the father, and so on. This coherence, these relationships involving both privileges and obligations, are gone too, says Donne. Each man now sets out to be a law unto himself. There has arisen an individualism which has disrupted the old hierarchical pattern. Every man thinks himself a phoenix. The phoenix was a fabulous bird believed in by the ancients. According to one version of the matter, a phoenix lived for five hundred years, after which it built itself a funeral pyre and died on it; and from its ashes a fresh phoenix arose. Thus at any given time there was only one phoenix in existence. Every man now, says Donne, considers himself a phoenix, considers himself unique, an isolated case, a law unto himself: every man now prefers to rely on his private judgment and not on authority. The subject no longer willingly submits, automatically, to the authority of the prince; the son no longer willingly submits, automatically, to the authority of the father. The old hierarchical pattern in human society is gone.

I have little doubt that Donne has in mind the idea that if you disrupt the universal pattern in the realm of astronomy, then the whole pattern of order will disappear in the universe—in the world of human society and elsewhere. It is the doctrine of correspondences. To Donne, *all* coherence is gone, *all* is cast in doubt. Again, according to the old order-picture, as we have seen, *relation* was a cardinally important conception. Everything was thought of in its relations to other things. Donne complains that now, with the New Learning, all relation is gone: each man now considers himself a unique, independent being, self-reliant, individualistic.

. . . . .

If we look in the field of Elizabethan drama for the most conspicuous example of a man who makes himself his own law, who is a super-individualist, who regards himself as a

phoenix, as it were, we shall probably fix on Marlowe's
Tamburlaine. He is the first of Marlowe's great studies in the
aspiring mind. Now in the two *Tamburlaine* plays there are
passages which momentarily suggest to our minds attitudes
to the hero which conflict with the overall attitude that Marlowe
wants us to take up towards him. For example, there are
passages in which the familiar theme of the Falls of Princes is
suggested. It is suggested that Tamburlaine at the height of
his astonishing career of conquest may come toppling down—
himself overthrown. The Falls of Princes was a favourite
medieval theme. But this momentarily suggested idea conflicts
with the predominating theme in the two plays: we are surely
intended by the author to regard the hero with imaginative
enthusiasm, and actually to approve of him.

In an interesting book on *Tamburlaine*, published in 1941
Mr. Roy W. Battenhouse indicates the way in which many
members of Marlowe's audiences in his own day doubtless
regarded the hero. Many, indeed most, people in Marlowe's
day would regard Tamburlaine as an evil man, as a man
whose aspiration was unwarrantable, wicked, presumptuous,
and whose methods were vile. It is true that what one may call
orthodox Elizabethan opinion would tend so to regard him.
For, despite Donne's pessimism in the passage which we have
examined, the fact is that the old order-philosophy fought
strenuously against the inroads of the new conceptions, and
it was not a minority which still clung to it. The upholding
of the old order-pattern is a most vital part of Renascence
mental activity.

Most members of Marlowe's contemporary audiences,
then, would, while they found Tamburlaine imaginatively
most impressive and exciting, disapprove of him with their
judgment. But I cannot follow Mr. Battenhouse when he
claims that Marlowe himself so regards his Tamburlaine. I
believe, with the majority of critics, that in these two plays
Marlowe *defies* the orthodox view of such a figure. With an
insolence which one must grant to be superb he sets his face
against the view that most of his contemporaries would take.
Marlowe is here a rebel against the order-picture.

In Tamburlaine, Marlowe presents, enthusiastically and

admiringly, the portrait of a man motivated by an aspiration which refuses any sort of control. Tamburlaine is self-confident, self-reliant, individualistic. He refuses to allow any subordination of himself. If Fortune and the gods are on his side and help him, as he tells us, yet elsewhere he tells us that he himself turns Fortune's wheel about, and again that he will war against the gods if necessary. He will have nothing to do with the picture of an ordered universe in which each created thing keeps to its own appointed place. He wants to soar above his own appointed place by his own efforts, forcibly. And Marlowe himself glorifies this.

If Tamburlaine's death at the end of Part II is a final defeat for him, it is nevertheless also a victory for him: for we are left with the idea that while on the one hand Tamburlaine himself goes on to a higher plane of existence, on the other hand his work on earth will be continued by his surviving sons—his own flesh embodying his own spirit—in other words, himself. Thus Death cannot in the last resort really defeat him.

It is true that Tamburlaine finds a justification for his colossal aspiration in an idea which belongs to the old order-pattern which had prevailed for so long. In the old order-pattern there were natural hostilities. It was believed, for instance, that in the human body the various elements were always struggling, each of them wanting to get control. The ideal state of affairs was a correct proportion amongst them in the body: but it was regarded as a matter of fact that each was always striving for mastery. And this was natural. In this idea Tamburlaine finds a justification for his ambition, which may even involve treachery: he justifies his treacherous treatment of Cosroe by saying that

> Nature, that fram'd us of four elements
> Warring within our breasts for regiment,
> Doth teach us all to have aspiring minds.
> (Part I, II, v i, 18-20).

But it is true also that Tamburlaine's aspiration and his methods in going about the realization of it are indebted to something that was not part of the old order-pattern, something new that conflicted with it. This is Machiavellianism. Tamburlaine uses Machiavellian methods, and in the two

D

plays these methods are held up to admiration by Marlowe.

Machiavelli (1469–1527), a Florentine statesman and political philosopher, wrote his best known work, *The Prince*, in 1513. It was printed in 1532. No English translation was published until 1640, but Machiavellian ideas were known in England long before that. Some English readers knew his work in the original. The Italian text was published in England in 1584. And translations existed in manuscript form.[1]

Machiavelli's face is set against the order-picture we have described, as it related to human society. By what means should a ruler govern? Professor Spencer points out that we may understand the answer given by those who upheld the order-pattern if we quote from Cicero's *De Officiis*. "According to Cicero," says Professor Spencer,[2] "if a man is to control his fellow men and himself, justice is the essential virtue, and moral right is the basis of action." He points out that Cicero regarded force and fraud as bestial and wholly unworthy of man.

Machiavelli on the other hand holds that the ruler must make use of force and fraud. Otherwise, men being what they are, he will not be able to rule at all. For to Machiavelli men are naturally evil and disorderly, and the best way to govern them for their own good is by force and fear. Government is not for Machiavelli based on any conception of universal justice. According to the doctrine of order, the government of a ruler should be a reflection of the government of God—the ruler corresponds to God, and must base his rule on universal justice. Machiavelli is against this idea, and so he is against the old order-pattern.

Those who upheld the doctrine of order would naturally disapprove of the writings of Machiavelli. The usual Elizabethan attitude to Machiavelli was one of hostility, because the influence of the order-picture was widespread and strong.

An Elizabethan who believed in the order-pattern, then, and who had read Machiavelli in the original, would tend to disapprove of him. It may be mentioned in addition that there

---

[1] See N. Orsini, *Journal of the Warburg Institute*, vol. I (1937), pp. 166–9.

[2] *Shakespeare and the Nature of Man*, p. 41.

was another reason for English disapproval of Machiavellian doctrines—a reason why people who had not even read Machiavelli in the original would disapprove of him, perhaps even more violently than those who had. In 1576 a French Protestant called Gentillet published a work, a *Contre-Machiavel*, containing translations into French of some of Machiavelli's political principles, with adverse criticism of them.

Gentillet considered Machiavelli an evil, an infamous, man. As a matter of fact he quite seriously misrepresents Machiavelli in his book, and the attack cannot be called a fair one. But it was an attack which influenced many Frenchmen and Englishmen in the latter part of the sixteenth century. Machiavelli was an Italian, and a Florentine to boot. In 1547 Catarina de' Medici became queen of France as consort of Henri II. She belonged to the resplendent Florentine family of the Medici. And, with her as queen of France, there sprang up a strong anti-Italian feeling in France. Italian adventurers crowded into the French court and were favoured by her. She gratified their avarice, and there was naturally resentment among the French. This aroused anti-Italian feeling, and this feeling helped to condition the French view of the Florentine writer Machiavelli.

Gentillet's book expresses this hostile view. To him Machiavelli belongs to a greedy and rapacious nation, and is a man whose political philosophy is repellent. Gentillet's book had a very great influence in helping to determine the Elizabethan view of Machiavelli. Dr. Mario Praz, in an important lecture on this subject,[1] has shown that the French attitude to Machiavelli had penetrated to Scotland even before the publication of Gentillet's book. "Therefore," he says, "we may safely conclude that Gentillet's book was not the sole source for the English travesty of Machiavelli. That book, certainly, did much towards giving wide circulation to the Machiavellian scarecrow, and fixing its abiding characteristics, but the ground on which it fell had already been prepared to receive it."[2]

[1] *Machiavelli and the Elizabethans*, printed in the 1928 volume of the *Transactions of the British Academy*.
[2] Op. cit., p. 7.

Now Marlowe's *Tamburlaine* is a Machiavellian figure, certainly. He is guided, as Mr. Battenhouse has shown,[1] by principles which Machiavelli himself actually advocated. The majority of the contemporary Elizabethan audience would disapprove of them. Mr. Battenhouse would have it that Marlowe disapproved of them also. But I think those are right who hold instead that Marlowe with grand insolence sweeps aside the orthodox Elizabethan view of these ideas and actually revels in them himself. It may be pointed out that the first part of *Tamburlaine* was an enormous popular success, this resulting in the writing of the second part, as is indicated in the prologue to the second part. But the fact that it was a popular success does not necessarily mean that contemporary audiences approved of the figure of the hero entirely as regards his aims and methods. They could find him imaginatively interesting and exciting even if they thought of him as essentially wicked. Marlowe, I am sure, meant him to be thought of as a magnificent and admirable figure.

Here, then, Marlowe glorifies a super-individualist—one who goes clean contrary to the old order-pattern, one who makes himself his own measure, one who rejects all notion of subordination as far as he himself is concerned. In his succeeding plays, it must be pointed out, Marlowe reverses the balance of his judgment.

In *Doctor Faustus* Marlowe works within the conception of the order-pattern, assuming its validity. Faustus aspires beyond what is legitimate for a human being and pays the penalty. Marlowe sympathizes with him, certainly, and in a way admires him: but his *judgment* of him is clear. The aspiring mind over-reaches itself, and Faustus, an imaginatively compelling hero, a tragic figure, is also presented as a fool. In *The Jew of Malta* Barabas is a super-individualist—he does not care for the welfare even of his fellow Jews so long as he himself can enjoy his wealth and prosperity. Marlowe's judgment is against him also, even though again there is a powerful imaginative appeal in the character. A powerful imaginative appeal does not necessarily imply an approval of him by the judgment of author or audience. We may think of

[1] *Marlowe's "Tamburlaine"*, pp. 206 ff.

Milton's Satan, or Shakespeare's Macbeth. Tamburlaine, then, is exceptional in Marlowe: in the plays about him the idea of the individual human being as the phoenix is upheld. With his judgment, after *Tamburlaine*, Marlowe may be said to have recanted. And in a case like Chapman's *Tragedy of Bussy D'Ambois* we have a Tamburlaine-figure who is, however, brought down by his own rashness and indiscipline. Behind all Chapman's tragic heroes, it has been said, "is the genuine problem of reconciling the highly prized liberty of the individual with the just claims of society."[1]

. . . . .

Shakespeare has his super-individualists too—men who, in order to fulfill themselves, act in such a way as to threaten, more or less seriously, the order-pattern. In *The Taming of the Shrew* we have a wife who aspires to independence of her husband—in the "great chain of being" she should accept the notion of obedience to him, subservience to him. In *Twelfth Night* we have in Malvolio a servant who aspires to become a count and whose blind self-love and unreasonable ambition make him a figure of fun. In the history plays we have rebellions against legitimate kings. In the tragedies we have people like Macbeth, a subject who by murder of his king makes himself king—people like Goneril and Regan, who, being daughters, behave towards their father in a way contrary to that in which daughters should behave towards their fathers according to the law of order. In *King Lear* we also have Edmund, another figure who contravenes the law of order so that he may further his own personal interests. And we have other examples. These characters are presented by Shakespeare very powerfully; they make a tremendous impression on our imaginations as we read or see. But we do not approve of them morally, nor does Shakespeare want us to. Shakespeare believes in the order-picture.

We have said that according to the order-conception order is natural, disorder unnatural. Again and again in Shakespeare and elsewhere we find the terms "nature" and "natural" applied to order-relationships. At the same time it must be

[1] Henry W. Wells, *Elizabethan and Jacobean Playwrights* (1939), pp. 86–7.

noted that, in *King Lear*, Edmund, a disorder-figure, invokes
Nature as his goddess. In the light of the order-conception
Edmund is an unnatural creature: but, as he reveals himself
to us as precisely that, he says:

> Thou, nature, art my goddess; to thy law
> My services are bound.
>
> (I, ii, 1–2)

That is, there are two distinct conceptions of Nature. According
to the one, she is a great integrating force, binding things
together in their due relationships. According to the other, she
is the force which inspires the super-individualist who brushes
the order-pattern aside.[1]

Shakespeare disapproves of the character who, in his own
interests, sets out to destroy the order-scheme. In all of his
plays he is concerned with the conceptions of order and
disorder: and for the most part he gives us a pattern in which,
a state of disorder having been produced, order is in the end
re-established.[2] Macbeth does not finally succeed, nor Edmund,
nor Iago. Lear may die: Othello may die: but the impression
we are left with at the end is that order has been restored in
the world. Goneril and Regan, Edmund, Iago—all are rejected
by author and audience. All the time Shakespeare is on the
side of order.

Earlier in this chapter we studied a quotation from John
Donne. He deplores the fact that the New Learning has broken
up the old order-picture of the universe. Some of the mental
activity of the Renascence was devoted to doing precisely that.
But some of the mental activity of the Renascence was
devoted to preserving the old order-picture: and it is here that
Shakespeare belongs. Shakespeare's universe is the Ptolemaic
universe. He holds no brief for the Machiavellian. He believes
in the order-scheme. He has no approval to bestow on the
Tamburlaine kind of individualist. He refuses to see man in
isolation: always he views him in relation to other men, in
relation to other planes of being. Shakespeare is not in doubt:

[1] On this, see John F. Danby's *Shakespeare's Doctrine of Nature: A
Study of "King Lear"* (1949) *passim*, and also Robert B. Heilman's *This
Great Stage: Image and Structure in "King Lear"* (1948), pp. 115 ff.

[2] We shall later on study an exception in *Troilus and Cressida*.

for him the element of fire is not put out: he knows where to look for the sun: he knows the true relationships of prince and subject, of father and son: the individual is not for him a phoenix: and for him relation and coherence are concepts of supreme validity.

. . .

One important aspect of the order-scheme remains to be mentioned. The individual human being was regarded as consisting of a number of parts hierarchically arranged. The body consisted of three main sections. The lowest, controlled by the liver, had to do with the vegetative side of man's existence. The middle part, controlled by the heart, had to do with the emotional aspect of his existence. The highest part consisted of the brain. The brain itself, to quote Dr. Tillyard, was "like the body . . . divided into a triple hierarchy. The lowest contained the five senses. The middle contained first the common sense, which received and summarized the reports of the five senses, second the fancy, and third the memory. This middle area supplied the materials for the highest to work on. The highest contained the supreme human faculty, the reason, by which man is separated from the beasts and allied to God and the angels, with its two parts, the understanding (or wit) and the will."[1]

Shakespeare deals not only with disordered environments but also with disordered people. In the correctly balanced man this elaborate hierarchy is maintained exactly as it should be—each part of the man occupies precisely its own position in the scale of his being. If any part gets out of its true relation to the others, then a disordered personality results. For example, the will is the faculty which makes a man do this rather than that. In the correctly balanced man the will accepts the recommendations of the understanding. If a particular man's will refuses to accept the recommendations of his understanding, then that man is psychologically deranged. Again, if a man's passions succeed in ruling him altogether, then we have a disordered personality. And a psychologically disordered person is likely to act in such a way as to produce disorder in his

[1] *The Elizabethan World Picture*, p. 65.

environment, or in such a way as to aggravate it if it exists already.

· · · · ·

The above account of this Shakespearian philosophy, a commonplace enough philosophy in his time, is simply a brief summary, and it is heavily indebted to the books I have mentioned. But it is everywhere in Shakespeare: the reader of Shakespeare *must* know something about it: and no book about Shakespeare can be of much help without some account of it. In the chapters which follow, it will be referred to again and again. It is basic.

wife corresponds to a rebellious subject. We may take the hint and go further. The sin of Satan was that he rebelled against God: a rebellious wife is acting correspondingly to that.

We have in Shakespeare's tragedies cases of transgression against the principle of order which have terrible consequences. Macbeth murders his king and usurps his place. And so on. There we are given by Shakespeare a vivid impression of the horror attendant on the destruction or attempted destruction of order. In *Macbeth* order is (temporarily) destroyed in such a way as to call forth from the audience an emotional response inappropriate to the dramatic genre we call comedy. In *The Taming of the Shrew* we have a play which is part romantic comedy, part farce. What Shakespeare emphasizes here is the foolishness of trying to destroy order, not the horror. "I am ashamed," says Katharine,

> that women are so simple
> To offer war where they should kneel for peace,
> Or seek for rule, supremacy and sway,
> When they are bound to serve, love and obey.
>
> (V, ii, 161-4)

The word "simple" means "foolish". It is the folly that Shakespeare stresses in the comedy, the horror in the tragedy. But the attempts of Katharine and Macbeth to destroy order *correspond*.

A moment ago we mentioned the sin of Satan. It resulted in dreadful consequences for mankind. His rebellion was an act that we must look upon with horror. But readers of Mr. C. S. Lewis's book *A Preface to "Paradise Lost"* (1942) are familiar with the idea that Satan's rebellion against God was foolish as well as evil. Mr. Lewis points out that Milton's poem can be fully understood only by those who realize that "it might have been a comic poem." Milton is writing an epic, and "has therefore subordinated the absurdity of Satan to the misery which he suffers and inflicts."[1] We look on Satan's rebellion with horror—we accord it the emotional response due to epic handling—Milton wants us to do that and makes us do that.

[1] Op. cit., p. 93.

But the informed reader realizes that, while he is concerned primarily with the horror of Satan's rebellion, it was
also absurd. Had it not been so dire in its results for mankind
it might well have been matter for comedy—the absurdity
might have been stressed rather than the horror. The absurdity
of Satan lies under the surface, as it were. Now in the case of
The Taming of the Shrew it is the other way about. We have
seen that when order was destroyed on one plane of reality
it was considered possible that there would be an associated
destruction of order on other planes of reality. The ultimate
result might be universal disintegration. This ultimate result
is nowhere even hinted at in *The Taming of the Shrew*. Shakespeare is writing a comedy. He is not concerned with horror.
He does not want to arouse in his audience emotions such as
are aroused by tragedy. But I have little doubt that the
sophisticated member of his contemporary audience would
say that this spectre of universal disintegration was there
hovering in the background, even in *The Taming of the Shrew*
For Shakespeare's contemporaries it was there, as an ultimate
most grievous possibility, since order had been assailed on one
plane of reality. But in the comedy this possibility is not
mentioned at all, for that would have destroyed the mood of
the play altogether. Order is established at the end before any
fundamental damage is done.

Shakespeare often thinks of disorder in terms of inversion—
the inversion of true relationships. In her final speech Katharine
indicates that we have been dealing with inversion: she is
ashamed that women are so foolish as

> To offer war where they should kneel for peace,
> Or seek for rule, supremacy and sway,
> When they are bound to serve, love and obey.
> (V, ii, 162–4)

We may compare in tragedy the terrible inversion principle
of the Witches in *Macbeth*: "Fair is foul, and foul is fair"—
and Satan's cry in Milton: "Evil, be thou my good!".

We may notice another passage in this final speech of
Katharine, a passage interesting because of its imagery. Having
exhorted Hortensio's wife to "unknit that threatening unkind

brow, And dart not scornful glances" at her husband, she goes
on:

> It blots thy beauty as frosts do bite the meads,
> Confounds thy fame as whirlwinds shake fair buds,
> And in no sense is meet or amiable.
> A woman moved is like a fountain troubled,
> Muddy, ill-seeming, thick, bereft of beauty;
> And while it is so, none so dry or thirsty
> Will deign to sip or touch one drop of it.
>
> (V, ii, 139–45)

In an important book entitled *The Shakespearian Tempest*
(1932) Mr. G. Wilson Knight shows how very frequently
Shakespeare conceives of peace and agreement in terms of
music played or sung in tune, and of disagreement and conflict
in terms of music out of tune. And he shows also how frequently Shakespeare conceives of conflict in terms of storm or
inclement weather, and of peace and concord in terms of fair
weather. And so we have an antithesis between tempest-
imagery and music-imagery (imagery relating to music in
tune), giving imaginative expression to the antithesis between
conflict and concord. The term "tempest-imagery" applies to
quite a large and varied body of imagery: when, following Mr.
Wilson Knight, we speak of a piece of "tempest-imagery",
we do not necessarily mean a piece of imagery directly related
to an actual storm; the term may be used of imagery relating
to any of the less agreeable aspects of nature. And when
Katharine speaks of the frown of a rebellious wife blotting her
beauty "as frosts do bite the meads", or confounding her fame
"as whirlwinds shake fair buds", we have tempest-imagery.
The idea it expresses is that of conflict—and, moreover,
unnatural conflict, disorder.

A true interpretation of *The Taming of the Shrew*, then,
depends on our considering it in relation to the doctrine of
order, the doctrine of the harmonious hierarchical universe.
Disorder is made to give way to order in one particular section
of human society, the domestic circle. The play is not a matter
of the disgusting triumph of a bully over a woman whose spirit
he breaks and who becomes miserably cowed. Katharine's
final speech is decidedly positive in tone, and delivered quite

definitely with spirit. And she has become a fountain of clea
water from which her lord can drink and find spiritual refresh
ment thereby. There is a beauty and a happiness in her lif
now that there was not before.

Most enlightened people nowadays do not think of marriag
altogether as Shakespeare thought of it. We think rathe
of partnership between equals. But the reader of *Th*
Taming of the Shrew must try to grasp the conception c
Shakespeare and his age and accept these imaginatively fo
the moment.

.   .   .   .   .

To turn to another comedy, we find at the beginning c
As You Like It a court environment in which order has bee
overthrown. The Duke Frederick has rebelled against hi
elder brother, the Duke Senior, has defeated him, driven hir
into exile, and usurped his domain. Here is a double atta
on the principle of order—a subject has rebelled against h
ruler, and a younger brother has behaved unnaturally toward
an elder brother. In this court circle we have another opponen
of order in the person of Oliver. He is treating his younge
brother Orlando unnaturally. As Orlando says, Oliver kee
him "rustically at home, or, to speak more properly, stays m
here at home unkept; for call you that keeping for a gentlema
of my birth, that differs not from the stalling of an ox? Hi
horses are bred better . . . He lets me feed with his hind
bars me the place of a brother, and, as much as in him lie
mines my gentility with my education" (I, i, 8–23).

Oliver does not treat Orlando as a brother should treat
brother according to the divinely established order of things
Oliver is trying to degrade Orlando from his proper statu
of gentleman to a status far below it—to the status of a peasan
("you have trained me like a peasant, obscuring and hidin
from me all gentleman-like qualities", I, i, 72–4) and even t
the status of an animal. Orlando himself is not at all to blame
He willingly accords Oliver all the privileges of his seniority
and, despite the wrongs he suffers, will not harm Olive
physically. Oliver's animus against him is a result of envy
He says that he does not know why he hates Orlando, an

hen proceeds to give the reason. "My soul," he says, "yet I
:now not why, hates nothing more than he. Yet he's gentle,
never schooled and yet learned, full of noble device, of all sorts
enchantingly beloved, and indeed, so much in the heart of the
world, and especially of my own people, who best know him,
hat I am altogether misprised" (I, i, 175–82). Compare the
Duke Frederick's reasons for driving Rosalind into exile. She
was kept at court when her father, the Duke Senior, was
banished, in order to be companion to Frederick's daughter
Celia. Frederick now drives her out also. Le Beau says that of
late the Duke Frederick

> Hath ta'en displeasure 'gainst his gentle niece,
> Grounded upon no other argument
> But that the people praise her for her virtues
> And pity her for her good father's sake.
>
> (I, ii, 290–93)

d Frederick himself says to Celia:

> her smoothness,
> Her very silence and her patience
> Speak to the people, and they pity her.
> Thou art a fool: she robs thee of thy name;
> And thou wilt show more bright and seem more virtuous
> When she is gone.
>
> (I, iii, 79–84)

he Duke obviously thinks of Rosalind as a danger to his own
usurped position (cf. I, iii, 60—"Thou art thy father's
daughter"), but there is envy involved also, I think, as there
certainly is in Oliver's case.

Shakespeare, then, gives us two parallel cases of opponents
of order—Frederick who injures his elder brother, and Oliver
who injures his younger brother. Shakespeare elsewhere
makes use of such parallelism. In *King Lear*, both Lear and
Gloucester err in trusting their elder offspring (two daughters
in the one case, one son in the other) and distrusting their
younger offspring. We may note also in passing that in
Orlando we have a case of a youth who, though he has been
denied the appropriate education and upbringing, shows the
qualities of mind and character appropriate to his station

("never schooled and yet learned, full of noble device")
Shakespeare apparently believes that, no matter how unfavourable the environment, the qualities one inherits will inevitably
assert themselves. Compare Guiderius and Arviragus in
Cymbeline. Though they have been brought up from childhood
in the Welsh mountains, unaware of their identity, living a life
entirely different from that at court, the mettle appropriate in a
King's offspring asserts itself in them by the force of nature.

The court milieu at the beginning of *As You Like It*, then,
is one in which disorder flourishes. Life in the forest of Arden
is contrasted with "that of painted pomp", with the perilous
life in "the envious court" (II, i, 3-4). This is the
"court versus country" theme which recurs in Shakespeare
in other plays. In *As You Like It* we have to deal with a
very serious degree of disorder in the court life. The
fidelity and conscientiousness of the old servant Adam are
contrasted by Orlando with the general rule that obtains in
this environment:

> O good old man, how well in thee appears
> The constant service of the antique world,
> When service sweat for duty, not for meed!
> Thou art not for the fashion of these times,
> Where none will sweat but for promotion,
> And having that, do choke their service up
> Even with the having: it is not so with thee.
>   (II, iii, 56-62)

And it is Adam himself who gives what is perhaps the most
striking evidence of the disorder that is rampant. Speaking to
Orlando he says:

> Know you not, master, to some kind of men
> Their graces serve them but as enemies?
> No more do yours: your virtues, gentle master,
> Are sanctified and holy traitors to you.
> O, what a world is this, when what is comely
> Envenoms him that bears it!
>   (II, iii, 10-15)

"Envenoms" means "kills by poison". In the true order of
things a man's graces and virtues should assist him in his

fe, but here a man's virtues are a danger to him, exciting the
envy of others. The true order of things is inverted. Compare
again in *Macbeth* the Witches' cry of "Fair is foul, and foul
is fair". A man's virtues are "sanctified and holy" things:
but, since they here constitute a danger to him, they are spoken
of in the passage as "sanctified and holy traitors". The
oxymoron helps to emphasize the state of inversion with
which we have to deal in the corrupt, disordered environment
of the beginning of this play.

We shall be concerned with *As You Like It* again later,
but it may be well to point out here that Shakespeare does not
believe that court life must necessarily be corrupt and disordered. In fact he is concerned in *As You Like It* to point
out by implication that escapism is no solution: at the end
of the play we have most of the exiles returning from the
forest of Arden, and we are clearly meant to understand that
the court environment has been rid of its evil. Disorder has
been set right.

.   .   .   .   .

In a volume of essays published in 1934, entitled *Determinations*,[1] there is a paper—*Notes on Comedy*—by Professor
L. C. Knights. He attacks the habit of generalizing as to the
nature of comedy. "Comedy," he says, "has provided a
happy hunting-ground for the generalizers. It is almost
impossible to read a particular comedy without the interference of critical presuppositions, derived from one or other
of those who have sought to define Comedy in the abstract."[2]
It is certainly undesirable that a reader should approach a
comedy of Shakespeare—or of any other dramatist—with a
preconceived idea of the essential nature of what he is going
to find. In such a case it is likely that he will read things into
Shakespeare's play, instead of letting the play speak for itself.
The same is true of tragedy, of course. The reader should
take each play as an entity in itself.

Nevertheless, if we read every play in the Comedies section
of the Shakespearian first folio, honestly trying to rid our

[1] Edited, with an Introduction, by F. R. Leavis.
[2] Op. cit., p. 109.

minds of presuppositions as to the nature of comedy, an
allowing each play to impact itself on our critical faculti
without the interference of such presuppositions, we cann
help noticing that various of the plays have various features
common. And it seems to me neither illegitimate nor profitle
to point these features out—provided that, having found the
in two or three or four plays, we do not proceed to a fifth in
state of determination to find them there also.

One of the generalizations about the nature of comed
which Professor Knights attacks is the view "that Comed
is a Social Corrective, comic laughter a medicine administere
to Society to cure its aberrations from the norm of Goo
Sense"; and he goes on to point out that "Meredith's cel
brated essay, in which this theory is embedded, has been
misfortune for criticism."[1]

Now it would certainly be a misfortune if a reader were
approach Shakespeare's comedies for the first time under th
impression that the *raison d'être* of these comedies—of a
comedies—is to correct the follies and vices of society. Und
these circumstances the reader is not likely to allow the pla
to speak for themselves. Nevertheless, if one reads them a
far as possible without presuppositions as to the nature
comedy, one actually finds that in those Shakespeare pla
called comedies in the first folio there is frequently a go
deal of criticism of follies and vices.

Shakespeare's comedies—all Shakespeare's plays—are, a
were intended by their author to be, works of art. The
evolution was controlled by Shakespeare's conscious artist
shaping power. And Shakespeare, not only artist but practic
man of the theatre, making his living by it, was, we may b
sure, very much concerned to entertain his audience—to gi
it pleasure. I do not suppose that in his comedies Shakespea
had social correction in his mind as his primary purpose. Bu
frequently the dramatic material which he used for artist
purposes, in order to entertain his audiences, was materi
which embodied social criticism—material which embodie
critical attitudes to various follies or vices, critical attitudes t
various ideals and ways of life. Shakespeare's comedies ar

[1] Op. cit., p. 111.

n fact, frequently *critical*. The material which Shakespeare
uses for dramatic, for artistic, purposes is material which
involves *as an essential part of its being* the weighing up and
assessing of different values, ways of life, etc. This is true
not only of the comedies but of all the plays. In this chapter,
however, we are concerned particularly with comedy.

We have already spoken of *The Taming of the Shrew*, in
which a wife is induced to substitute obedience to her husband
for insubordination, and in which she explicitly states, towards the end, the "moral" of the play. The relation of wife
to husband is in this play viewed in the light of a complete
conception of the nature of the universe. The play is essentially
concerned with this conception of the universe as related to a
particular section of it—the relation of wife and husband.
To say this is not to deny that it is also concerned with two
vivid personalities (and with other personalities also, more or
less vivid). But it is essentially concerned with morality and
with metaphysics. Wrong conduct in Katharine is exposed as
wrong, right conduct is shown to be right; and it is all connected with the doctrine of universal order. Obviously the
play is essentially critical.

If we take another early comedy, *Love's Labour's Lost*, we
find that we are dealing with the critical assessment of different
theories of living"[1] and also with contemporary personages
who held them. The play is topical to a degree, and if the
reader does not realize this he misses a good deal of the fun
which the play involves. A perusal of Miss Frances A. Yates's
book, *A Study of "Love's Labour's Lost"* (1936), brings us into
contact with a whole gallery of sixteenth-century names in
connection with the play—John Florio, John Eliot, Gabriel
Harvey, Thomas Nashe, Sir Walter Raleigh, George Chapman,
Giordano Bruno, and others. The unravelling of some of the
mysteries of the play in the light of Miss Yates's researches
may seem to be just an academic exercise, unnecessary for the
general reader who just wants to enjoy the play whether or not
he fully understands it. And it must be admitted, as Miss
Yates herself admits, that there are elements of conjecture in
her book—elements of doubt. But she is certainly on the right

[1] See M. C. Bradbrook, *The School of Night* (1936), p. 161.

lines, and if one follows her as she builds up her case one
finds the play taking on a greater vitality than one might
otherwise be aware of.

The play is concerned with various "designs of life"
with various "theories of living", and with contemporary
personages who held them. If the detecting of the personages
that Shakespeare has in mind is an intricate business, it is
at any rate, quite obvious from the play itself what the main
"theories of living" are. They are not only exhibited; they are
assessed. The play is again *critical*.

We find contrasted on the one hand a particular kind of
contemplative scholarly life, and on the other hand the active
life of the lover. At the outset, the King of Navarre and three
of his attendant lords are seen about to embrace for three
years a life of arduous study, withdrawn from the affairs of
the world—a life without physical comforts, and a life in which
they will have nothing to do with women.

One of the young lords, Berowne, though agreeing to
adopt this way of life along with the others, has much to say
against it. For one thing, he argues that they will find it
impossible to remain true to their vow of having nothing to
do with ladies. A man's emotional being is an essential part
him and he cannot simply set it aside by force, as it were. This
is what this plan involves: the young men are proposing to
allow their intellects full sway and to set aside their passion
their emotional life. One cannot do this simply by willing to
do it, says Berowne: it can be done "by special grace" (pro
bably the reference here is to religious asceticism), but that
is not involved here. Thus self-deception is involved in the
plan (time and again in his plays Shakespeare exposes self
deception). But even if this academic asceticism were possible
for them, it would be a bad thing—so Berowne holds. The
type of scholarly activity that is being proposed is, he holds
arid. One reads and reads—one reads oneself blind, without
attaining the light of wisdom. What is involved is pedantry—
the fruitless activity of the "continual plodder" who simply
learns what other people have said. Such bookworm knowledge
does not enlarge their personalities or enrich their lives. The
pedant actually cuts himself off from life. As Miss Yates says

Berowne is very far from wishing to exalt stupidity and ignorance. He does not despise knowledge, but he assimilates thoroughly into his personality. Learning is not something into which he retreats as an escape from life, but something which he carries with him into life . . . The play is thus a reiteration of a truth which wise men in all ages have always emphasized, that a man must be large enough to absorb and digest his learning, to make it one with himself, to experience it as something which applies to life as he knows it."[1]

It is the acquiring of knowledge in a vacuum—the scholar moving away from life—that Berowne objects to. Against this kind of life he sets the active life of the lover. The lover does not try, as the pedant does, to suppress part of his personality. Love, unlike pedantry, develops the whole personality. "Other slow arts", says Berowne,

> entirely keep the brain;
> And therefore, finding barren practisers,
> Scarce show a harvest of their heavy toil:
> But love, first learned in a lady's eyes,
> Lives not alone immured in the brain;
> But, with the motion of all elements,
> Courses as swift as thought in every power,
> And gives to every power a double power,
> Above their functions and their offices.
> It adds a precious seeing to the eye; etc.
>
> (IV, iii, 324–33)

Love enriches the lover's life—pedantry does not enrich the pedant's life. As Miss Yates says, "Shakespeare's plea for life is a plea for the right kind of love, that rational love between the sexes the search for which was a most noble contribution of the Italian Renaissance towards the civilizing of mankind."[2] Love confers on the lover a wisdom which sterile book-learning does not confer on the "continual plodder".

> Small have continual plodders ever won
> Save base authority from others' books.
>
> (I, i, 86–7)

[1] Op. cit., pp. 196–7.
[2] Op. cit., pp. 197–8.

In the Renascence period there were prevalent two sharp contrasted attitudes to love and women. On the one hand woman was almost deified and love was glorified (the Petrarchian attitude); on the other hand woman was contemned and love debased (the anti-Petrarchian attitude). The controversy between the Petrarchists and the anti-Petrarchists is mirrored in *Love's Labour's Lost*. Though agreeing to retire with Navarre and the others into their "little academe," Berowne from the beginning argues for the life of the lover as opposed to that of the pedant: but paradoxically at the start Berowne is an anti-Petrarchist. When he falls in love (despite himself) with his Rosaline, he turns from an anti-Petrarchist into a Petrarchist *par excellence*, and his defence of love takes on a note of greater personal conviction.

There can be no doubt that in presenting this play Shakespeare wants his audience to reject the life of the pedant and believe in the validity of the life of the lover. It is true that at the end he presents to us yet another kind of life. The young men, having declared their love to the ladies, are told by them that they cannot have their hands in marriage until a year has passed. The King of Navarre is told by the Princess of France that he must

> go with speed
> To some forlorn and naked hermitage,
> Remote from all the pleasures of the world . . . .
> (V, ii, 804–6)

If his love for her survives this, then at the year's end he shall have her. Berowne is told by Rosaline that he must

> this twelvemonth term from day to day
> Visit the speechless sick and still converse
> With groaning wretches; and your task shall be,
> With all the fierce endeavour of your wit
> To enforce the pained impotent to smile.
> (V, ii, 860–64)

The life of the lover is not *rejected* by Shakespeare in favour of the life of the Christian hermit or the visitor of the sick. The young men are to have the ladies in the end. But this conclusion gives us Shakespeare's last word against the life of he pedant: if a man *does* retire from the world and shut himself up, then it should not be to live the life of a pedant—it should be to live the virtuous life of a hermit. As Miss Yates puts it, "If the world is to be renounced, Shakespeare seems to say, it must be from motives of love and pity, not of cold intellectual exclusiveness and pride."[1]

It will be seen, then, that in order properly to understand *Love's Labour's Lost* one must know something about Shakespeare's contemporaries and about the ideas they held concerning life and how it should be lived. But the main point I want to stress here is that the play is critical: Shakespeare deals with "theories of living"—he assesses them—he rejects one conception of life, he accepts another. One simply cannot read or watch the play without finding oneself involved not only in an inspection of different ways of life but in an assessment of them. Criticism is an essential element in the play. Shakespeare is not writing a tract or preaching a sermon: the play is not "didactic" in the sense in which that word is usually employed. But as he writes for our delectation—in order to give us aesthetic pleasure—he presents dramatic material which actually embodies a vision of what is a valid and spiritually profitable life and what is an invalid and spiritually unprofitable life.

. . . . .

If we pass to more mature Shakespearian comedies we find this same element of criticism. Consider *Twelfth Night*. Here we have a number of self-deceivers of different kinds, and they are exposed as such. We have the Duke Orsino, in love with Olivia—or so he thinks. He is an example of the stereotyped aristocratic forlorn lover. Olivia will have none of him, and his psychological condition and his behaviour are conventionally appropriate to this situation. He is in a state of voluptuous love-melancholy. He likes to listen to love-music, and he enjoys the scent of "sweet beds of flowers": love-thoughts, he says,

> lie rich when canopied with bowers.
>
> (I, i, 41)

[1] Op. cit., p. 199.

He is certainly in love with his condition—with that, one ma
say, rather than truly with Olivia. He likes solitude in th
conventional fashion: "I myself am best," he says, "Whe
least in company" (I, iv, 40–1). "How does he love me?
asks Olivia of the disguised Viola: and the reply gives a tru
picture of the conventional forlorn lover:

> With adorations, fertile tears,
> With groans that thunder love, with sighs of fire.
> (I, v, 274–5)

Orsino himself says that

> such as I am all true lovers are,
> Unstaid and skittish in all motions else,
> Save in the constant image of the creature
> That is beloved.
> (II, iv, 17–20)

He is constantly talking of the overwhelming strength of hi
passion: and to him Olivia is a "sovereign cruelty". He lose
no opportunity of declaring that his love is insatiable. In short
he is the conventional aristocratic disdained lover. In *Twelft
Night* this conventional love-psychology and love-behaviour
is satirized—it is good-natured, certainly, but it *is* satire. I
is social corrective. We certainly have to do with satire whe
Viola, speaking on behalf of Orsino, addresses Olivia a
"Most radiant, exquisite and unmatchable beauty" (I, v, 181)
and then breaks off to ascertain that the lady she is addressin
really is Olivia, for she would be loth to waste her speech—
"besides that it is excellently well penned, I have taken grea
pains to con it."

The effect of this is to convey to the audience a satiric
impression of Orsino's love, Viola acting as Orsino's ambas-
sador. On a later embassage on Orsino's behalf, Viola says to
Olivia "Most excellent accomplished lady, the heavens rain
odours on you!" (III, i, 95), and so on: and Sir Andrew
Aguecheek's delighted approval of her diction underlines the
satire, for there must surely be something wrong with anything
that that egregious fool approves of so admiringly. In Act II,
scene iv, Orsino asks again for

> That old and antique song we heard last night.
> (II, iv, 3)

It is the tenderly melancholy song "Come away, come away, death . . . I am slain by a fair cruel maid." Orsino revels in the mood of the song, which is sung by Feste, the jester: and after it Orsino wants to be alone with his delicious melancholy—he says to Feste, "Give me now leave to leave thee" (II, iv, 74). And Feste rounds on him with some very direct criticism:

> Now, the melancholy god protect thee; and the tailor make thy doublet of changeable taffeta, for thy mind is a very opal. I would have men of such constancy put to sea, that their business might be every thing and their intent every where; for that's it that always makes a good voyage of nothing.
>
> (II, iv, 75–81)

Feste here attacks Orsino for his lack of mental stability. His mind is an opal—the opal is iridescent, changes colour as the light falls on it from different directions. Orsino's mind has a similar inconstancy. Such a man should wear shot silk, which is also iridescent, not of a single colour. Such a man, if he put to sea, would bring his expedition to nought for lack of firm purpose. Such a mentality simply will not do in this life. Here we have Feste criticizing Orsino, satirizing him, the conventional forlorn lover. And Feste is an example of the wise fool who perceives and comments upon the folly of allegedly wise men. If it were not clear from the portrait of Orsino itself that Shakespeare was satirizing the conventional forlorn lover, Feste's direct comment would indicate that to us. The wise fool acts as commentator for the dramatist. Orsino is the conventional disdained lover: and it is clear that he is not in love with Olivia so much as (to use a rather trite phrase) in love with being in love; so that he is a self-deceiver.

Olivia too is presented as a romantic sentimentalist. She has but lately lost her brother by death. On account of her sorrow, and to keep her love for him lasting, she has vowed that for seven years she will lead a cloistered existence, abjuring the sight of men. She will have nothing to do with lovers—in particular with Orsino. Now this cloistral attitude of Olivia is presented as a piece of sentimental affectation. We have seen how Feste, the wise fool, criticizes Orsino's romantic sentimentalism: he also criticizes Olivia's:

> *Feste.* God bless thee, lady!
> *Olivia.* Take the fool away.
> *Feste.* Do you not hear, fellows? Take away the lady.
>
> (I, v, 41–4)

Feste sees clearly that Olivia's role as the inconsolable sister is a foolish pose; his voice is the voice of common sense as he declares "As there is no true cuckold but calamity, so beauty's a flower" (I, v, 56–7). This contains a warning to Olivia that female beauty is of short duration—"beauty's a flower": she should therefore accept love before it is too late, before her beauty fades and no lover will have her; beauty being so transient, one cannot afford to waste time in an affected keeping of love at arm's length.

And Feste sees also that Olivia is deceiving herself. She has vowed herself to a celibate cloistral existence: but very soon we are to see her falling in love with Cesario and throwing herself at him in flagrant contradiction of her vow. Feste early foresees that something like this will happen. "There is no true cuckold but calamity," he says. By vowing herself to her cloistral existence Olivia has married calamity; but calamity is a cuckold, a husband whose wife is unfaithful to him: that is to say, Olivia will be unfaithful to her vow. Feste foresees this. He realizes that in taking her vow Olivia was duping herself—thwarting her real inclinations and adopting a romantic pose.

Feste is not Olivia's only critic. The first words we hear from Sir Toby Belch are a criticism of the course she is taking, which conflicts with the kind of life for which Sir Toby stands, the life of jollity and good fellowship. "What a plague means my niece," he says, "to take the death of her brother thus? I am sure care's an enemy to life" (I, iii, 1–3). She is voluntarily keeping sorrow alive, which to Sir Toby is a foolish and unnatural thing to do.

And Olivia is criticized by Viola, too. Viola realizes that Olivia is deceiving herself. "I prithee," says Olivia (III, i, 150), "tell me what thou think'st of me." And Viola replies, "That you do think you are not what you are." That is precisely Olivia's trouble. Viola also criticizes Olivia on a moral ground. "Lady," she says,

> you are the cruell'st she alive,
> If you will lead these graces to the grave
> And leave the world no copy.
>
> (I, v, 259–61)

"No copy"—that is, no child who will survive after her. To
remain unwed and childless would be cruel, and more than
cruel, immoral. "Are you the lady of the house?" asks Viola at
I, v, 198. "If I do not usurp myself, I am," replies Olivia.
"Most certain," retorts Viola, "if you are she, you do usurp
yourself; for what is yours to bestow is not yours to reserve."
To refuse to bestow her love on a man is to fail in her duty as
a woman: it is immoral.

Olivia's affectation, then, is criticized adversely by Feste,
by Sir Toby, and by Viola. Before long Olivia abandons the
pose. She falls violently in love with Cesario. But there is
manifest irony here. For her abandonment of the pose is
caused by her falling in love with a person she cannot possibly
have, since "he" is actually a girl; and, following from this,
when Olivia falls in love with Cesario, *she*, Olivia, has to take
the initiative, reversing the normal order of things. She has
to make the advances. As far as *she* knows, she has fallen in
love with a young man and is, by his indifference and by the
strength of her own feelings, impelled actually to pursue
him; and she is well aware that this is dishonourable and
wrong:

> I have said too much unto a heart of stone
> And laid mine honour too unchary out:
> There's something in me that reproves my fault;
> But such a headstrong potent fault it is,
> That it but mocks reproof.
>
> (III, iv, 221–5)

She has abandoned one wrong attitude only to take up another
wrong attitude.

Now, of course, it would be quite wrong to say that, in
Twelfth Night, Shakespeare condemns romantic love. Romantic
love emerges triumphant in the end. But, as Shakespeare
works out his romantic main plot, he directs shafts of criticism
against Orsino's and Olivia's self-deception and sentimental

posing—posing which is part of the romantic love convention. You can criticize something without desiring to destroy it in its entirety. And so here in *Twelfth Night* we have Shakespeare criticizing the sentimentalists, criticizing, in Sir Edmund Chambers's words, "the tendency of minds pent in the artificial atmosphere of cities to a spiritual self-deception, whereby they indulge in the expression of emotions not because they really have them, but because they have come to be regarded by themselves or others as modish or delightful emotions to have."[1]

But this is not all the social criticism in the play. There is the sub-plot with, among others, Sir Andrew Aguecheek and Malvolio. *Twelfth Night* is, as regards these two characters at any rate, a very Jonsonian play. This is shown in detail by Mr. Paul Mueschke and Miss Jeannette Fleisher in a paper published in 1933.[2] They show that Sir Andrew resembles Stephen, the country gull, in *Every Man in his Humour*. And Professor O. J. Campbell calls Sir Andrew "Shakespeare's composite of Matthew and Stephen, Jonson's city and country gulls."[3] He goes on: "He is derided, exposed, and ejected from the company of the wise and the sane, as are all ridiculed figures in satire of any sort. But Shakespeare's lampooning of Sir Andrew is utterly devoid of malice."

Malvolio, a much more complex figure than Sir Andrew, is also a Jonsonian character. He also is satirized, criticized, by Shakespeare. He is a "humour" character. In Elizabethan physiology the humours were fluids present in the body, four in number—choler, melancholy, phlegm, and blood. Jonson uses the term metaphorically, as he explains near the beginning of *Every Man out of his Humour*:

> So in every human body
> The choler, melancholy, phlegm, and blood,
> By reason that they flow continually
> In some one part, and are not continent,
> Receive the name of humours. Now thus far

[1] *Shakespeare: A Survey* (1935), p. 174.
[2] *Publications of the Modern Language Association of America*, Vol. 48 (1933), pp. 722 ff.
[3] *Shakespeare's Satire* (1943), p. 83.

It may, by metaphor, apply itself
Unto the general disposition:
As when some one peculiar quality
Doth so possess a man, that it doth draw
All his affects, his spirits, and his powers,
In their confluxions, all to run one way,
This may be truly said to be a humour.

Malvolio exemplifies the humour of self-love or pride. Olivia says to him, "O, you are sick of self-love, Malvolio, and taste with a distempered appetite" (I, v, 99). That is the key to Malvolio—he is sick of self-love. And his self-love, or pride, causes him to defy the principle of degree of which we have spoken—Malvolio wishes to climb above his station—he wishes to marry Olivia—he, the steward, to marry with the countess. Not only so, but he is a self-deceiver, and fancies that the countess is in love with him. Despite the tendency of some critics to sentimentalize him, to argue that Shakespeare has a lurking sympathy for him (I cannot believe that he has much, if any), we must say that Malvolio is in the play satirized as one afflicted with the humour of self-love, a social climber, and a self-deceiver. The self-deceiver falls a ready victim to the trickery of Sir Toby and his associates.

Malvolio stands in sharp contrast to Sir Toby. They dislike each other intensely, and this is a vital part of Shakespeare's design in *Twelfth Night*. Sir Toby believes in a life of ease and gaiety, jollity, good fare and merriment. In Act II, scene iii, we see Malvolio trying to put a stop to a carousal involving Sir Toby and his friends. Malvolio stands in opposition to the way of life that Sir Toby represents and believes in. It has been suggested that the ground of Malvolio's opposition to Sir Toby's way of life is puritanism.[1] I cannot agree that Shakespeare is concerned, or at any rate primarily concerned, to show Malvolio as a Puritan. He comes in to put a stop to the carousal on Olivia's behalf. She disapproves of Sir Toby's way of life. Why? Partly because it conflicts with her romantic pose as the inconsolable sister. Partly, I think,

[1] See A. H. Tolman, *Falstaff and Other Shakespearean Topics* (1925), pp. 146-51.

for another reason, which is suggested by Professor John W. Draper.[1]

He points out that Sir Toby and Malvolio are retainers of Olivia's, but retainers of very different types. Sir Toby is a retainer of a type which by Shakespeare's time was fast becoming anachronistic. He is descended from the armed retainers necessary in former times in noblemen's castles when these noblemen might at any moment become involved in private warfare. Such armed retainers, as Professor Draper says, "feasted in the hall, brawled in doors and out, and scorned all servile duties."[2] But by Shakespeare's day the social conditions which made such retainers necessary were passing. To quote from Professor Draper again: "The end of private warfare had brought the nobles out of their castles into the more convenient confines of the Tudor house. They no longer required a host of idle men-at-arms, and could not easily maintain them. Servants became more purely useful . . . Lord Burghley advised his son to keep few servants, and give them not only board and lodging but also wages regularly paid. Thus the household was evolving from a feudal to an economic basis . . . Elizabethan servants, employed more and more for work rather than prowess, were 'passing from a condition of status to one of contract'; Shakespeare would seem to have transferred to Illyria a household in the midst of this transition, with a licensed 'fool', well-born retainers, dependent relatives and uninvited guests as in the Middle Ages, and also apparently with a staff of actual servants headed by the all-too-competent Malvolio, who could not but look askance at the free and easy manners of the rest."[3]

Olivia opposes Sir Toby's way of life, then, first because it conflicts with the austerity laid upon her by her romantic pose as the inconsolable sister, and secondly because Sir Toby is a type of retainer who is not only unnecessary but expensive. Malvolio opposes Sir Toby and his way of life first because Olivia does, and he wants to stand well with her, and secondly because there is in any case an antipathy between the two

[1] See *Publications of the Modern Language Association of America*, Vol. 49 (1934), pp. 797 ff.
[2] Op. cit., p. 798.
[3] Op. cit., pp. 799-800.

types of retainer. Sir Toby, well-born, looks down on Malvolio: "Art any more than a steward? Dost thou think, because thou art virtuous, there shall be no more cakes and ale?" (II, iii, 122–5). Malvolio, foolishly and presumptuously looking forward to becoming the husband of Olivia, takes great pleasure in dreaming of the day when he will be able to lord it over Sir Toby and reprove him for his riotousness from a station higher than Sir Toby's own.

There is no doubt that Shakespeare deeply sympathizes with Sir Toby's way of life. Sir Toby's way of life is in conflict with Olivia's romantic pose—Shakespeare criticizes her romantic pose. Sir Toby's way of life comes into conflict with the more economical life in which he is an anachronism and servants of the Malvolio type are requisite. Shakespeare's sympathies appear to be with the former. Can one doubt, having read the play, that Shakespeare thinks that "cakes and ale" are good things?

And yet—finally—consider the impression made upon us by the last sight of Sir Toby that we get in the play. Malvolio is by the end thoroughly exposed as presumptuous, foolish, and a self-deceiver. And he is not cured of his humour of self-love. But what of Sir Toby? If Shakespeare really approves of what Sir Toby stands for, as I think he undoubtedly does, it nevertheless remains a fact that our last impression of Sir Toby is of a distinctly disreputable and down-at-heel old rascal. He enters limping (V, i, 196)—he is in need of the help of a surgeon (but the surgeon is drunk)—Sir Andrew offers to help Sir Toby, but Sir Toby rounds on him with "Will you help? an ass-head and a coxcomb and a knave, a thin-faced knave, a gull!" which is not very pretty—and he is hurried off to bed on Olivia's orders. The impression we get is, as I say, of a disreputable, down-at-heel, old rascal.

For Shakespeare's satire, as we find again and again, is often the reverse of simple. He will hold up to ridicule one way of life or one person, upholding against it another way of life or another person; but then we find that this other way of life or person is also satirized. It is frequently with Shakespeare far from a matter of simple blacks and whites. He can condemn some things unequivocally—as, for example, he

condemns the life of the bookworm isolated from life in
Love's Labour's Lost, or as he condemns the presumptuous
fool Malvolio in *Twelfth Night*. But on the other hand, having
held up as on the whole valid a certain way of life, he can turn
round and point out that after all there may be something
wrong with that, too. In the same way in the midst of a piece
of satiric portraiture, Shakespeare can put in a little touch
that gives us a momentary impression of pathos which implies
a touch of sympathy or at any rate pity; as, for example, where
we have this piece of dialogue:

> *Sir Toby.* She's a beagle, true-bred, and one that
>   adores me: what o' that?
> *Sir Andrew.* I was adored once too.
>
> (II, iii, 195-7)

In the essay to which we have already referred, Professor
L. C. Knights, speaking specifically of the *Henry IV* plays,
says: "Now satire implies a standard, and in *Henry IV* the
validity of the standard itself is questioned; hence the peculiar
coherence and universality of the play. 'Honour' and 'state-
craft' are set in opposition to the natural life of the body, but
the chief body of the play is, explicitly, 'a bolting-hutch of
beastliness'."[1] This is a very true observation. We shall consider the *Henry IV* plays in due course.

Meanwhile, I would point out that this design, which
Professor Knights rightly points to in these plays, is a design
that Shakespeare uses elsewhere also. He more than once
takes one way of life and criticizes it by contrasting it with a
second way of life: but then we find that he also criticizes
that second way of life. He may go on to delineate a third
way of life, consisting of an amended version of the first,
the amendment being due to the influence of the second.
This is what he does in *As You Like It*, another comedy in
which he is concerned with social criticism, and with the
order-disorder antithesis.

In the comedies we have so far looked at Shakespeare
concerns himself with exposing follies. In *As You Like It* he
does this, too; but here he also concerns himself with vice,

[1] *Determinations*, pp. 128-9.

with evil. We have already seen that the court environment to which we are introduced at the beginning of the play is one in which disorder is rampant; a subject has dispossessed his ruler; in two cases a brother has behaved unnaturally towards a brother; men's virtues are their enemies; and so on. It is a disordered environment, and the disorder springs from evil. We have seen also that life in the forest of Arden is set in contrast with this corrupt court life. It is a case of a favourite Shakespearian theme—that of court *versus* country.

In the first scene of the play Oliver asks Charles the wrestler "Where will the old duke live?" And Charles replies:

> They say he is already in the forest of Arden, and a many merry men with him; and there they live like the old Robin Hood of England: they say many young gentlemen flock to him every day, and fleet the time carelessly, as they did in the golden world.

(I, i, 120–5)

By "the golden world" is meant the Golden Age, the reign of Saturn on earth, when men lived in a state of ideal happiness and prosperity. There was no conflict, no war, no weapons. Man's food was brought forth from the earth without his having to labour to get it. "Perpetual spring reigned, flowers sprang up without seed, the rivers flowed with milk and wine, and yellow honey distilled from the oaks."[1]

Now many readers and critics speak as if life in Shakespeare's forest of Arden were, in fact, nothing but idyllic pleasure, happiness, ease, comfort, jollity. When we ourselves get into the forest, at the beginning of Act II, we quickly find that it is by no means altogether that. And when we look attentively at the passage in Act I which we have quoted, spoken by Charles the wrestler, we notice the twice repeated formula "they say". The account of life in the forest of Arden that Charles gives us is the account that is going round the court. It is based on rumour, hearsay. We are supposed to take it that the forest is a long way from the court. Sir Arthur Quiller-Couch points out that "all the fugitives reach this

---

[1] C. M. Gayley, *The Classic Myths in English Literature*, 1896 edition, p. 43.

F

Forest of Arden leg-weary and almost dead-beat. Sighs
Rosalind, 'O Jupiter! how weary are my spirits!' invoking
Jupiter as a Ganymede should. Touchstone retorts, 'I care
not for my spirits, if my legs were not weary'; and Celia
entreats, 'I pray you, bear with me, I cannot go no further':
as, later on, old Adam echoes, 'Dear master, I can go no
further'; and again, we remember, Oliver arrives footsore,
in rags, and stretches himself to sleep, so dog-tired that even
a snake, coiling about his throat, fails to awaken him. It is
only the young athlete Orlando who bears the journey well.''[1]

Now Shakespeare may well have a symbolic purpose here:
the forest of Arden is a place of spiritual refreshment—these
people have come from an environment of disorder and evil—
their need of spiritual refreshment is symbolized by their
physical fatigue. But even if this is in Shakespeare's mind,
we are entitled to interpret on a realistic plane as well. Admitting
that Rosalind and Celia are girls and Adam almost an octo-
genarian, so that their fatigue need not be particularly significant, and admitting that Touchstone, the court fool, who,
as we find in the play, likes physical comfort, may not be in
the best of physical trim, there is the fact that even Oliver is
exhausted when he gets to Arden. Arden is a long way from
the court, and the journey is a hard one. When the idea
of going to Arden is suggested to Rosalind in the first place
she says:

> Alas, what danger will it be to us,
> Maids as we are, to travel forth so far!
>   (I, iii, 110–11)

Reverting to Charles's report of what life in the forest is like,
we can be quite sure that whoever started the rumour had
not trudged the long way there to see, and the long way back
to report what he had seen. Charles's report is hearsay, and
when we get into the forest ourselves we find that it is not in
all respects accurate.

The first scene which takes place in the forest is II, i. At
the beginning of this scene the exiled Duke speaks to his
fellows:

[1] The New Shakespeare: *As You Like It* (1926), p. ix.

Now, my co-mates and brothers in exile,
Hath not old custom made this life more sweet
Than that of painted pomp? Are not these woods
More free from peril than the envious court?
Here feel we not the penalty of Adam[1]
The seasons' difference?—as the icy fang
And churlish chiding of the winter's wind,
Which, when it bites and blows upon my body,
Even till I shrink with cold, I smile and say
'This is no flattery: these are counsellors
That feelingly persuade me what I am.'

(II, i, 1–11)

What he asks in line 5 is—do we not here in Arden suffer those afflictions to which all men as such are subject, and only those afflictions, not the sort of man-made afflictions one has to suffer in the "envious court"? He contrasts the life in Arden and the life in the envious court very pointedly. At court there is "painted pomp", there is envy, flattery, and so on; it is a dangerous life (but, we may say, though it is only implied, not stated, in the passage, there are physical comforts at court). Here in Arden the moral atmosphere is pure—one does not have to put up with the evil that prevails at court: but there is little physical comfort here in Arden. The Duke uses words which are incisive—he means what he says: he speaks of "the icy fang" and the "churlish chiding" of the winter wind—"fang" is a very meaningful word; he speaks of the wind "biting" his body and of himself "shrinking" with cold, and we feel that the words themselves have bite. We have just got into the forest, and Shakespeare takes care to make us fully aware at the very start that this is a place where life is physically difficult, in contrast to life at court. Life in Arden is hard, physically uncomfortable, *but* the moral atmosphere is pure; life at court is physically comfortable, *but* the moral atmosphere is corrupt, evil.

If we do not realize the physical hardship of life in Arden, then we do not appreciate the distinction between Arden and the court in all its fullness: we blunt an essential point in the play. The Duke Senior speaks of Arden as "this desert city" (II, i, 23): and it is interesting to observe how often this word

---

[1] This line is as in the "New Shakespeare" edition.

"desert" is used by those who come to Arden. It may be pointed out that in Shakespeare's day this word could be used to indicate simply an unfrequented place, as opposed to a town or city. But in *As You Like It* we observe that words such as "wild", "abandoned", "uncouth", and "savage" are used in connection with the forest. In II, vi, Orlando calls it "this uncouth forest" and a little later "this desert". In II, vii, he speaks of "this desert inaccessible", and he says: "I thought that all things had been savage here". In V, iv, Jaques de Boys speaks of "this wild wood" and the melancholy Jaques speaks of the Duke Senior's "abandon'd cave". "Uncouth", "savage", "wild", "abandoned"—the impression that such words are intended to convey is quite clear.

We have this fundamental antithesis, then, between Duke Frederick's court where there is physical comfort but moral corruption, and the forest of Arden where there is physical discomfort but moral purity. It is an antithesis between an evil life and a good life; but the matter is not just so simple as that.

The forest of Arden has its critics within the play. The melancholy Jaques is one of them. In II, v, Amiens sings the song "Under the greenwood tree", lyrically glorifying the life in Arden:

> Here shall he see
> No enemy
> But winter and rough weather.

And Jaques proceeds to parody the song:

> If it do come to pass
> That any man turn ass,
> Leaving his wealth and ease,
> A stubborn will to please,
> Ducdame, ducdame, ducdame:
> Here shall he see
> Gross fools as he,
> An if he will come to me.

(II, v, 52–9)

According to Jaques, the Duke Senior and the others are gross fools to have left the wealth and ease of their former life at court and to have accepted instead the rigours of life in Arden.

Now it is unquestionably true that Shakespeare satirizes Jaques in the play: but Touchstone also criticizes Arden. "Well", says Rosalind on their arrival, "this is the forest of Arden." "Ay," replies Touchstone, "now am I in Arden; the more fool I; when I was at home, I was in a better place: but travellers must be content" (II, iv, 15–18).

This is the attitude of the Fool in *King Lear* also. Having rejected the homes of his unnatural daughters, Lear is out on the heath, with the Fool. And the Fool's attitude is that "court holy-water in a dry house is better than this rain-water out o' door" (by "court holy-water" he means the well-sounding but empty promises that people make to each other at court). According to the Fool in *Lear* "he that has a house to put's head in has a good head-piece" (III, ii, 10, 25). That is Touchstone's view in *As You Like It*.

Now Touchstone and the Fool in *Lear* are both, like Feste in *Twelfth Night*, examples of the wise fool—the fool who can often see truth when supposedly wiser men deceive themselves. But in connection with Touchstone and the Fool in *Lear* we must be careful. The words they speak in the passages just quoted are not meant by Shakespeare as a full statement of the attitudes he wants us to take up. Shakespeare is not saying to us in either *As You Like It* or *King Lear* that a life of ease which involves corruption is actually better than a physically hard life which does not involve corruption. The truth which Shakespeare wants us to extract from those words of Touchstone and the Fool in *Lear* is simply that there is something to be said against fleeing to Arden, there is something to be said against going out into the storm. Touchstone and the Fool in *Lear* see that. We are meant to see it. Touchstone's criticism of Arden is valid to that extent. But we are not meant to accept as desirable the evil that the Duke Senior and his friends have escaped from.

As regards the antithesis between the corrupt court of Duke Frederick and the forest of Arden, we are, as we have said, expected to take Arden as morally a better place. But, having established that, Shakespeare very quickly lets us see that there are things to be said against Arden. When you are faced with a corrupt world, Shakespeare seems to say in this play, you should not just run away from it and stay away from it. At the end we have most of the courtier-inhabitants of Arden returning home, and we have the definite prospect of a purification of the court environment itself, the inspiration for the purification having been supplied by the moral atmosphere of Arden. Arden justifies itself by virtue of the fact that it does supply that purifying inspiration.

The villainous Oliver and Duke Frederick both come to Arden with hostile intentions, and both are there converted from their evil thoughts and ways. Oliver is saved by Orlando from dangers of the forest. Orlando has always behaved towards Oliver as a brother should behave towards a brother, but this had never had any salutary effect on Oliver until now in the forest of Arden. I think that Shakespeare means us to regard it as significant that this conversion of Oliver takes place in Arden—Arden is the morally pure place where such conversions naturally happen. Duke Frederick comes to Arden with a force of soldiers, intending to kill his brother: on the very skirts of the forest he meets with "an old religious man" and is converted from his enterprise. Again, I think that Shakespeare means us to take it as significant that this happens in this place, in Arden. The atmosphere of Arden, then, suggests purification. But that purification should, and must, be applied to the world outside it. Escapism is condemned in this play.

Now, while we are in the forest of Arden we hear a great deal about love, that so frequent theme of Shakespearian comedy. Arden is the place where Silvius and Phebe live, and in them we have reflections of the conventional figures of Arcadian love-literature. Silvius is the adoring shepherd, Phebe the disdainful shepherdess. And they are both satirized. Silvius is a self-deluder. Phebe herself reproves him for uttering love-conceits of the conventional kind. Silvius tells her such things as that her eyes will kill him—a conceit of old vintage (compare Chaucer's "Your yen two wol slee me sodenly"). Phebe herself brings the light of cold fact to bear on this, exposing it as a foolish fiction—"there is no force in eyes That can do hurt" (III, v, 26-7). But Phebe too is a self-deluder. She affects disdainfulness, she puts on airs; but she has little call to do so—she is not by any means so beautiful as she (or Silvius) thinks, and Rosalind, speaking words of true wordly-wisdom, bids her accept a husband while she has a chance—"Sell when you can: you are not for all markets" (III, v, 60)—not everyone would have her. Rosalind chides them both for self-deception and tells them to face *facts*. To her Silvius is a "foolish shepherd":

> 'Tis not her glass, but you, that flatters her.
> (III, v, 54)

And to Phebe she recommends self-knowledge:

> But, mistress, know yourself: down on your knees,
> And thank heaven, fasting, for a good man's love.
> (III, v, 57–8)

Self-delusion is exposed to the light of down-to-earth common sense. And Touchstone is in agreement with Rosalind in this. The Jane Smile whom Touchstone professes in II, iv, to have loved once, and the Audrey whom he takes in marriage in the forest of Arden, may be crude and unlovely creatures, but they are at least *real*. The lover Orlando, too, is good-naturedly satirized in Arden—the lover who affixes rather poor love-verses to the barks of trees. In the forest of Arden, then, we have the pastoral love scene, and we have the extravagances and sentimentalities and illusions of conventional pastoral love exposed by having the standards of real-life common sense applied to them.

It must be pointed out that Shakespeare is not against romantic love as such, nor does he mean that all men should marry women like Jane Smile and Audrey. It is the extravagances and foolishnesses common amongst some romantic lovers that he satirizes. He attacks the unrealities in the minds of foolish romantic lovers. Jane Smile and Audrey are real. But they are not the only reality. Romantic love purged of extravagance and foolishness is to Shakespeare a fine thing. In this play, romantic love triumphs in the end. It may be pointed out that in the masque of Hymen we have something about as conventional as it might well be. But Shakespeare has made his point, and he can allow himself and his audiences the pleasure of a formal, artificial, but quite beautiful and amusing finish.

In *As You Like It*, then, we again have a Shakespearian comedy which is critical. Both vice and folly are exposed for what they are. And the tissue of criticism is quite complicated. Its complicated nature may be further exemplified by noting the fact that while, as we have seen, the moral atmosphere in Arden is pure, yet Arden is also the home of the shepherd Corin's master who is a man

> of churlish disposition
> And little recks to find the way to heaven
> By doing deeds of hospitality.
>
> (II, iv, 80–2)

And if Touchstone satirizes Arden, he also satirizes the court—

> I have trod a measure; I have flattered a lady; I have been politic with my friend, smooth with mine enemy; I have undone three tailors; I have had four quarrels, and like to have fought one.
>
> (V, iv, 45–9)

Again and again we find in dealing with Shakespeare's comedies that we are not dealing in simple blacks and whites. A person or a way of life may be criticized by a standard which is itself then found to be open to criticism. As regards *As You Like It*, it is, I think, fair to say that one way of life (the court life at the beginning) is criticized by a comparison with a second way of life (that in the forest of Arden): but that is in its turn criticized, and what emerges at the end as the dominant impression is a third way of life consisting of an amendment of the first (the purified court), the amendment being due to the influence of the second.

CHAPTER IV

IMAGINATIVE INTERPRETATION AND *TROILUS AND CRESSIDA*

THERE is a kind of interpretation of Shakespeare's work advanced by some nowadays (though by others aspersed) which is called "Imaginative Interpretation" by one of its principal exponents, Mr. G. Wilson Knight.[1] Mr. Wilson Knight was the pioneer in this field, and others have followed him. Mr. T. S. Eliot approves of his methods,[2] and similar methods are used by Professor L. C. Knights[3] and others.[4]

I confess to finding it distinctly difficult in a small book such as this, addressed primarily to the non-specialist, to do anything like justice to Mr. Wilson Knight's views. Many people would call them esoteric. To attempt a brief summary of them seems to me hazardous. For Mr. Wilson Knight is concerned with the very heart of the reality we call poetry, or rather with the very heart of poetic drama; and it is fair to say that his work may strike many as abstruse. He is concerned with interpretation which tries to state in intellectually understandable terms fundamental Shakespearian imaginative concepts.

It may be best to begin by remembering that many of us—probably—were brought up by teachers who, in studying Shakespeare with us, invited us to write essays and examination

---

[1] See, among Mr. Wilson Knight's works, *The Wheel of Fire* (1930), *The Imperial Theme* (1931), *The Shakespearian Tempest* (1932), and *The Crown of Life* (1947).

[2] See Mr. Eliot's Introduction to *The Wheel of Fire*.

[3] See Professor Knights's essay *How Many Children Had Lady Macbeth?* (1933), reprinted in his book *Explorations* (1946).

[4] One of the most recent pieces of "imaginative interpretation" of Shakespeare that I have seen is Professor Robert B. Heilman's *This Great Stage: Image and Structure in "King Lear"* (1948).

answers on Shakespeare's *characters*. "Write an essay on th
character of Hamlet." "Compare the characters of Jaques an
Hamlet." And so on. Criticizing the excessive preoccupatio
with *characters* in themselves, Professor L. C. Knights quote
various writers who speak of Shakespeare giving us in hi
plays characters who are credible in terms of real life. Amon
others he refers to Mr. Logan Pearsall Smith's book, *O
Reading Shakespeare*. "Here," says Professor Knights,[1] "Shake
speare is praised because he provides 'the illusion of reality'
because he puts 'living people' upon the stage, because h
creates characters who are 'independent of the work in whic
they appear . . . and when the curtain falls they go on livin
in our imaginations and remain as real to us as our familia
friends'." Dr. Knights goes on to point out that the "mos
illustrious example is, of course, Dr. Bradley's *Shakespearea
Tragedy*." Dr. Bradley is, in Dr. Knights's view, excessivel
preoccupied with the characters in Shakespeare's tragedies
He thinks of these characters as if they were, in fact, actua
real-life figures. "In the Lectures on *Macbeth* we learn tha
Macbeth was 'exceedingly ambitious. He must have been s
by temper. The tendency must have been greatly strengthene
by his marriage.' But 'it is difficult to be sure of his customar
demeanour'. And Dr. Bradley seems surprised that 'Thi
bold ambitious man of action has, within certain limits, th
imagination of a poet'. These minor points are symptomatic
It is assumed throughout the book that the most profitabl
discussion of Shakespeare's tragedies is in terms of th
characters of which they are composed."[2] Bradley's *Shake
spearean Tragedy* appeared in 1904. Since then, I imagine
most students of Shakespeare have read it at school o
university or both.

The group of critics with which we are here concerne
deplores the segregation of the characters as focal points o
interest. These critics, or interpreters, are concerned with th
reader's total response to the experience of a work of art o
which plot and characters are only portions. A Shakespearia
play, they point out, embodies a "poetic vision": the

---

[1] *Explorations*, p. 3.
[2] Ibid.

nterpreter should attempt to grasp that poetic vision. It will 1ot, I think, be giving a false impression to say that this school >f criticism regards a Shakespeare play as having what Mr. 3. L. Bethell calls a "hidden meaning"—it has "a significance)eyond the mere story and characters in themselves."[1] If this s putting the matter rather simply, it will, nevertheless, ndicate to the general reader the sort of view with which we ure dealing. Shakespeare embodies in a play a poetic vision— he reader must try to grasp that poetic vision. He must not solate the story, or isolate the characters, and think of them us having an existence independent of that poetic vision. Critics like Bradley, according to this school, do isolate the characters and think of them as if they were real-life figures. They are not concerned, as they should be, with the total response to the poetic drama.

Mr. Wilson Knight objects to this sort of character-criticism. He does not approve of the consideration of Shake-spearian characters in themselves. Nor does he approve of the consideration of the plot in itself. The plot of a play exists temporally. It consists of a sequence of events. But to Mr. Wilson Knight a Shakespeare play has also a "spatial" existence. That is to say, as he explains, there is, in a Shake-speare play a constant "atmosphere" which remains the same throughout. What he means will perhaps be best conveyed here by an example. In *Troilus and Cressida* there is, in his view, an opposition between "intuition", represented by the Trojans, and "intelligence", represented by the Greeks. This intuition-intelligence opposition is "active within and across *Troilus and Cressida*"; the opposition between the two conceptions exists "independently of the time-sequence which is the story". It encompasses the whole play: it exists spatially, to use Mr. Wilson Knight's metaphor. And it gives the temporal sequence, the story, its real significance. Isolate the story from this constant "atmosphere" and you will be isolating one element from the whole, and falsifying.

Or take another example. In *Antony and Cleopatra* we have a contrast between Egypt and Rome. Mr. Bethell regards

[1] See Mr. Bethell, *Shakespeare and the Popular Dramatic Tradition* 1944), p. 114.

this as the same contrast between intuition and intelligence
that we have just seen claimed in *Troilus and Cressida*. Or
Antony and Cleopatra, Mr. Bethell comments: "Egypt and
Rome are . . . opposed throughout the play: they represent
contradictory schemes of value, contradictory attitudes to
and interpretations of, the universe . . . Egypt and Rome
stand respectively for love and duty, or for pleasure and duty,
or even love-pleasure and duty."[1] This Egypt-Rome opposition
is the "atmosphere" of *Antony and Cleopatra*. To Mr. Wilson
Knight and his followers the "atmosphere" of a play is of vital
importance. It gives the play its most fundamental significance.

Mr. Knight, we have said, objects to character-criticism.
He also objects to criticism in the light of the author's intentions. In his view, the author's conscious intentions may
actually "prefigure a quite different reality from that which
eventually emerges in his work."[2] The author may produce
something different from what he consciously intended to
produce, and it is with what he produced and not with what
he intended to produce that the reader or spectator should be
concerned. What should matter to us is the pattern that
emerges from the play itself as we apprehend it imaginatively,
not what Shakespeare wanted his audience to experience.

Again, Mr. Wilson Knight rejects as invalid the study of
sources as an aid to interpretation. As he sees it, the poetic
dramatist finds a pre-existent tale useful—even necessary—
as a vehicle for the conveying of his vision: but the true source
of the play is his vision. "The 'source' of *Antony and Cleopatra*," says Mr. Knight, "if we must indeed have a 'source'
at all, is the transcendent erotic imagination of the poet which
finds its worthy bride in an old world romance."[3] Shakespeare
chooses a ready-made plot which accords with his poetic
vision: he embodies the vision in that plot, modifying the
plot according to the demands of the vision. But—as we have
said—he may not himself be fully aware of what the emergent
pattern of the play will be. He may not fully realize the
implications of his own vision.

---

[1] Bethell, op. cit., p. 122.
[2] *The Wheel of Fire*, ed. 1937, p. 7.
[3] Ibid., p. 9.

As regards what Mr. Bethell calls "hidden meanings", Mr. Wilson Knight points to various "values" to which Shakespeare gives expression in his plays. "By 'values'," he says, "I mean those positive qualities in man, those directions taken by human action, which to the imaginative understanding clearly receive high poetic honours throughout Shakespeare."[1] For example, he quotes passages "idealizing both kingship and 'honour'." Another Shakespearian "value" is love. Again, the "value" of order is vitally important in Shakespeare. And so on. Shakespeare is in his plays vitally concerned with such "values". They may be assailed by "negations"—love by hate, order by disorder, and so on. Thus, in interpreting a play, in trying to describe in intellectually comprehensible terms the poetic vision, we may find ourselves speaking in abstract terms, speaking of war, and kingship, and soldiership, and horsemanship, and order, and love, and hate, and disorder, and death, etc. Such things are the important thematic elements.

Now, I believe that Mr. Wilson Knight's work is of very great importance. I believe that when one takes up a play for study one should always turn to Mr. Knight to discover his interpretation of it, as well as turning to commentators whose methods are different. I have no doubt whatever that Shakespeare is concerned with the various values that Mr. Knight enumerates: I have already heavily emphasized the order-disorder antithesis which seems to me ubiquitous in Shakespeare. I have referred to the "tempest-music" antithesis which Mr. Knight rightly regards as fundamental. I agree wholeheartedly that a Shakespeare play is a work of art embodying a poetic vision. I believe that Mr. Knight's work is often extremely helpful and illuminating.

At the same time there are things about it that trouble me somewhat. Mr. Knight criticizes adversely those writers who, preoccupying themselves with plot and characters, appear to him to be dealing with things artificially abstracted from the totality of the play—things that have no real existence at all, only the totality having real existence. But I wonder if he himself does not also deal with things artificially abstracted

[1] *The Imperial Theme*, ed. 1939, p. 1.

from the whole. Professor L. C. Knights, himself an admirer of Mr. Wilson Knight's methods, himself voices this objection. His recent volume, *Explorations*, contains among other things a reprint of his essay entitled *How Many Children Had Lady Macbeth?* In the preface to the volume, Professor Knights writes thus, speaking of this essay: "The second half shows clearly an extensive indebtedness to the early work of Mr. Wilson Knight. Time has confirmed the impression I registered then (in a note omitted from the present reprint), that 'a preoccupation with imagery and symbols, unless minutely controlled by a sensitive intelligence directed upon the text, can lead to abstractions almost as dangerous as does a preoccupation with "character".' But a recognition of the limitations of Mr Knight's highly personal method should not be allowed to obscure the genuine original insight contained, in good measure, in *The Wheel of Fire* and *The Imperial Theme*." Professor Knights realizes that there is not "only one 'right' approach to each and all of" the Shakespearian tragedies. There is a sound point here. Mr. Wilson Knight's interpretations, in many cases most admirable as they are, may appear to some readers to be concerned no less than Bradley's with artificial abstractions from the whole play. In a given play we may say, with Mr. Knight, that Shakespeare is concerned with a particular positive assailed by a particular negative, the positive triumphing in the end; but we may also say that, being concerned with this, Shakespeare also concerns himself, *no less essentially*, with the fact that under certain circumstances a human being or a certain character behaves in such and such a way, or with the fact that in this life accident sometimes plays an important part in a man's fate. I cannot help believing that while admittedly a Shakespeare play is not just "a slice of life", while admittedly Shakespeare does not always give us plot-sequences likely to happen in real life or psychology consistent with real-life experience, while admittedly he is writing poetic dramas, while admittedly he is concerned with "themes", "symbols", "poetic vision", yet he *is* also, at the same time, concerned to present a story and characters.

The story *may* be such as could happen just so in real

ife; if not, the audience is induced to suspend disbelief and think of it as happening in real life. The characters *may* be such as are credible in terms of real-life psychology; if not, the audience is again induced to suspend disbelief. As we sit in the theatre and watch Othello being duped by Iago, we *do* think of them as human beings, we *do* think of them as reflecting real life, we *do* think of them as "characters". That does not mean that the "inner meanings" are not also present. Mr. Bethell suggests that "the exotic and sensual *Antony and Cleopatra* might . . . yield its hidden meaning to an audience simultaneously aware of the two levels of story and significance."[1] Professor H. B. Charlton has recently published a volume entitled *Shakespearian Tragedy* (1948). In the introduction he refers to the fact that "in the field of interpretation, the most striking trend of the last generation has been the assault on Andrew Bradley."

Professor Charlton assails the Wilson Knight school of interpretation, and says this: "When I am told that to attain the 'soul-experience' of a Shakespeare play is 'a process which forces us to cut below the crust of plot and character, and to expose those riches of poetic imagination too often buried in our purely unconscious enjoyment of Shakespeare's art,' I applaud the recognition of the mystery of poetic genius, but ask whether the crust has not itself some meaning, whether in fact it is not the means to meaning chosen by the poet, whether it be not indeed part of the form which has attained identity with its substance."[2] With this I heartily agree. I always recommend my students to read both Wilson Knight and Bradley. Professor Charlton declares himself to be "a devout Bradleyite". If we cannot all say quite that, I think we ought all to allow that there is still much that is most helpful in Bradley. "The crust has itself some meaning," even if from time to time Bradley thought *too* closely in terms of real-life psychology.

"The crust has itself some meaning." Rejecting character-criticism, Mr. Wilson Knight says, "So often we hear that in *Timon of Athens* it was Shakespeare's intention to show

[1] Op. cit., p. 114.
[2] Op. cit., p. 2.

how a generous but weak character may come to ruin through
an unwise use of his wealth'; that 'Shakespeare wished in
Macbeth to show how crime inevitably brings retribution'
that, 'in *Antony and Cleopatra* Shakespeare has given us a
lesson concerning the dangers of an uncontrolled passion'."
"These," Mr. Knight goes on, "are purely imaginary examples
coloured for my purpose, to indicate the type of ethical
criticism to which I refer."[1]

Now I am quite sure that, were it possible for us to
interrogate Shakespeare, he would tell us that, for example
in *Twelfth Night* he *was* concerned, *among other things*, with the
fact that in this life people sometimes adopt romantic poses—
they deceive themselves—and that is foolish. He would tell
us that in *The Taming of the Shrew* he *was* concerned, among
other things, with the fact that in this life a wife should behave
in such and such a way, and not otherwise. He would tell us
that in *Othello* he was concerned with a man of a certain
character, situated in certain circumstances, who is led by
both factors in conjunction into evil in thought and deed.
Mr. Knight may say that Shakespeare's intentions are irrelevant to a full and true experiencing of the play. I cannot
be sure of this. I think that Shakespeare generally knew what
he was doing, not just what he wanted to do. If it is said
that neither he nor any artist necessarily conveys his poetic
vision fully or exactly, that he even distorts it as his conscious
shaping power casts it into artistic form, I should reply
that what audience and readers are concerned with is
the vision as modified by the artist's conscious intentions.
I believe that our aim should be to go through and
enjoy an aesthetic experience as near as we can get to
that which the author wanted his audiences to go through
and enjoy.

Deploring character-criticism, Mr. Knight declares that
"the critic who notes primarily Macbeth's weakness is
criticizing him as a man rather than a dramatic person."
And again: "By noting 'faults' in Timon's 'character' we are
in effect saying that he would not be a success in real life,
which is beside the point, since he, and Macbeth, and Lear

---

[1] *The Wheel of Fire*, ed. 1937, pp. 9–10.

are evidently dramatic successes."[1] If by "dramatic successes" Mr. Knight means that these dramatic figures are so handled by Shakespeare as to produce in his audience a feeling of profound aesthetic satisfaction, we must most certainly agree that they are dramatic successes. Of course they are. But one may make a dramatic success out of a play which displays as hero a man whose character has certain weaknesses—weaknesses with which the dramatist is very much concerned. Richard II, for example, is a weak man. He is not a success as king. Shakespeare goes to a good deal of trouble to demonstrate his weakness of character. He even makes an explicit statement, through the Duke of York, of what is primarily wrong with Richard—in him "will doth mutiny with wit's regard" (II, i, 28). Everything in the play conduces to show that this is a correct psychological judgment of Richard. In the correctly balanced man the will accepts the guidance of the "wit" or understanding or judgment or reason; but not in Richard. He is a disordered personality, and that is why he is not a success as king. Shakespeare is, I have not the slightest doubt, under the impression that he is dealing with and explaining a man who actually lived and was not a success in actual life for this psychological reason.

I have already said that sometimes Shakespeare goes contrary to the psychological facts of real life in his plays: but sometimes he reflects them accurately: and always he is concerned with characters who give, at any rate, the illusion of being real-life figures. Timon, and Macbeth, and Lear *have* "faults" in their "characters", and Shakespeare deliberately emphasizes them. Lear is a man who "hath ever but slenderly known himself" (I, i, 297); again, "The best and soundest of his time hath been but rash" (I, i, 298). Everything in the play accords with this character-description, and there is no dramatic reason why Regan and Goneril should, in these lines, be deceiving themselves or us. Shakespeare deliberately interprets Lear psychologically. He *has* a fault in his character. Most human beings have faults in their characters, and Shakespeare is concerned to show us, in action, human beings or what look like human beings.

[1] *The Wheel of Fire*, ed. 1937, pp. 11-12.

G

Professor Charlton declares himself, as we have seen, to be "a devout Bradleyite". He describes Bradley's method thus: "He comes to the plays as a psychological naturalist, or rather as a natural psychologist. He sees the men who move through them as if they were real human beings struggling through a world which seems in moral substance very much like our own. He finds that the sequence of action by which they move to their destiny appears as the intelligible outcome of the particular impulses and motives which give to each of them his distinctive personality, and which operate within these characters as mankind's accumulated experience of humanity has found them tend to operate in real life. So Bradley is preoccupied, though not exclusively occupied, with Shakespeare's portrayal of his hero's character as an autonomous dynamic element, forging that man's future in its interplay with fate and circumstance."[1]

And Professor Charlton also says: "The public by pleasing whom Shakespeare lived, the public which is still pleased by Shakespeare, is sufficiently agreed in knowing what it means by a play. To them it is a theatrical and literary (often poetic) creation which represents action on a stage. The actors representing it look like men and women; they talk and speak like men and women; they encounter predicaments and respond to them variously, but more or less as such men and women as they shew themselves to be would respond in that sort of predicament. Moreover they exist in an imaged but visibly presented world not alien in essence from our own, and one in which the compelling forces, human and non-human, are not different in nature from the operative powers which we take to be the arbiters of our own human destiny in this our own world."[2] I should say that this is admirable, allowing that (a) there are greater and less degrees of psychological realism in Shakespeare's plays, and even within the same play, his art being *partly* non-naturalistic, and (b) the "inner meanings" *do* exist, though to isolate them to the exclusion of character and plot is to be guilty of artificial abstraction just as much as if it were the other way about.

[1] Op. cit., p. 4.
[2] Ibid., p. 6.

I hope it is clear that I believe that Mr. Wilson Knight's work has great value for the student of Shakespeare, though I think his methods have to be used with caution. The inner meanings do exist, though not to the exclusion of the sort of meaning with which critics of the Bradley school concern themselves. On the other hand, criticism of the latter kind is not sufficient in itself.

But now I must go on to declare that, while, as regards the inner meanings, there are cases in which I agree with Mr. Knight, there are other cases where I cannot but feel that his interpretations are not on the right lines. I propose to examine *Troilus and Cressida*, which is a case in point. But, of course, the fact that one disagrees with him in the interpretation of this or that particular play does not mean that one disagrees with his method *in toto*.

74367

As we have seen, Mr. Wilson Knight finds in *Troilus and Cressida* an antithesis between "intuition", represented by the Trojans, and "intelligence", represented by the Greeks; and, according to his view, we react with enthusiasm to the Trojan value and not to the Greek. The one is to be accepted, the other rejected. I cannot think that this is a correct view of the matter.

The love story is placed in the setting of the Trojan War, and as regards the war there is manifest disorder on *both* sides, Greek and Trojan.[1] In the earlier acts of the play we are presented with two conferences, one in the Grecian camp (I, iii), the other in Troy (II, ii). In these conference scenes the disorder on both sides is made very clear. Let us look at the Greek conference first.

It is here that Shakespeare gives us his most *explicit* statement of the doctrine of degree. Ulysses, who is presented as a reasonable man, a wise man, a discerning man whose diagnoses are likely to be correct, indicates what is wrong on the Greek side. Troy would already have been sacked, Hector

---

[1] It should be mentioned at the outset that I am aware of a considerable debt to Professor O. J. Campbell's book *Comicall Satyre and Shakespeare's "Troilus and Cressida"* (1938).

would already have been slain, had it not been that the Greek warriors have not paid due respect to the principle of degree. They have not properly subordinated themselves to Agamemnon, the commander-in-chief. Ulysses describes Agamemnon as the

> nerve and bone of Greece,
> Heart of our numbers, soul and only spirit,
> In whom the tempers and the minds of all
> Should be shut up.
>
> (I, iii, 55–58)

But the Greek chieftains are not treating him as that. The various chieftains are insisting on their own individualism. The Greek army is full of factions. "And, look," says Ulysses,

> how many Grecian tents do stand
> Hollow upon this plain, so many hollow factions.
>
> (I, iii, 79–80)

The principle of order, of degree, is observed, for example, by bees: but it is not observed here, and the result is that the Greek military effort is being frustrated:

> When that the general is not like the hive
> To whom the foragers shall all repair,
> What honey is expected?
>
> (I, iii, 81–83)

What is wrong in the Greek host is a very simple matter—for a military expedition to be successful everyone should subordinate himself unquestioningly to the commander; but here everyone seems to be out for himself only. And Ulysses, in his famous 'degree' speech, relates this disorder to the total conception of a disordered universe. The ultimate consequence of disorder in the universe is a ghastly outcome indeed:

> Take but degree away, untune that string,
> And, hark, what discord follows! each thing meets
> In mere oppugnancy: the bounded waters
> Should lift their bosoms higher than the shores
> And make a sop of all this solid globe:
> Strength should be lord of imbecility,
> And the rude son should strike his father dead:

Force should be right; or rather, right and wrong,
Between whose endless jar justice resides,
Should lose their names, and so should justice too.
Then every thing includes itself in power,
Power into will, will into appetite;
And appetite, an universal wolf,
So doubly seconded with will and power,
Must make perforce an universal prey,
And last eat up himself. Great Agamemnon,
This chaos, when degree is suffocate,
Follows the choking.

(I, iii, 109–26)

In the Greek camp, then, there is individualism among the chieftains instead of a total subordination to the commander-in-chief; there are factions instead of an ordered, united effort: degree is disregarded, and so the Greeks are having no success.

Ulysses goes on to indicate that Achilles is the principal offender. He has grown "dainty of his worth" (line 145), i.e. he has grown very particular about his own individual merits and about his own individual value to the Greek host. He is not content to execute his own functions under the commander-in-chief: he has become obsessed with his own prestige as the mightiest warrior among the Greeks, and he will not co-operate with the others. He lies in his tent mocking at the official plans for carrying on the siege (lines 145–6); he enjoys himself watching Patroclus guying Agamemnon and others. Insubordination—individualism in a subordinate—that is the disease, and it springs from the sin of pride (that is clear). Furthermore, we are told, Achilles' example has infected Ajax too, and others. Ajax "keeps his tent" like Achilles, "makes facetious feasts; rails on our state of war" (line 191), and encourages the scurrilous Thersites to speak foully of the other Greek heroes.

Ulysses tells us that the matter is not simply one of insubordination, though that in itself is bad enough. These disorder-figures among the Greeks object to military prudence—all that they value is the flamboyance of physical warlike action itself. They have no use for careful calculation, prudent planning, staff work: all that they consider worth while is the fighting itself:

> They tax our policy, and call it cowardice,
> Count wisdom as no member of the war,
> Forestall prescience and esteem no act
> But that of hand: the still and mental parts,
> That do contrive how many hands shall strike,
> When fitness calls them on, and know by measure
> Of their observant toil the enemies' weight,—
> Why, this hath not a finger's dignity:
> They call this bed-work, mappery, closet-war;
> So that the ram that batters down the wall,
> For the great swing and rudeness of his poise,
> They place before his hand that made the engine,
> Or those that with the fineness of their souls
> By reason guide his execution.
>
> (I, iii, 197–210)

The attitude of these traducers of degree, then, is contrary to reason. We might fairly say that they believe in the external glories of chivalric action in war, the picturesque splendour of sword-play: they do not believe in guiding the military exploit by the light of reason. Mr. Wilson Knight holds that the Greeks in this play symbolize intellect, reason. Ulysses does, certainly: but we are explicitly shown that not all the Greeks do—these disintegrators do not, obviously. Indeed, it is clear that the Greek forces are permeated by a spirit of unreason: that is the burden of Ulysses' remarks. And we may mention here also that the theme of love is relevant to the Greeks as well as to the Trojans. Agamemnon says:

> And may that soldier a mere recreant prove,
> That means not, hath not, or is not in love!
>
> (I, iii, 287–8)

And, as we shall see, the action of the play is affected by a love-affair involving Achilles.

Turning now to the council in Troy in II, ii, we find two schools of thought among the Trojan heroes concerning the war. The situation in this scene is that the Greeks have made an offer—if the Trojans will deliver up Helen, the war will be ended and no reparations will be demanded at all. This offer is discussed by the Trojans. And the debate develops into a contest between those who are guided by reason and those who are guided by honour. Hector starts the discussion by

voting "Let Helen go" (line 17). Helenus supports him.
Troilus and Paris oppose this. Troilus argues passionately
against the criterion of reason: it is contrary to the conception
of honour.

> Nay, if we talk of reason,
> Let's shut our gates and sleep: manhood and honour
> Should have hare-hearts, would they but fat their thoughts
> With this cramm'd reason: reason and respect
> Make livers pale and lustihood deject.

                                                    (II, ii, 46–50)

The antithesis between the reason-value and the honour-value
is clear. Hector points out that Helen is not worth "what she
doth cost The holding" (lines 51–2). Troilus replies "What is
aught, but as 'tis valued?", arguing for a purely subjective idea
of value. Hector replies that if a man considers something
positively valuable it must not be a case simply of subjectivism;
there must be some inherent quality in the object to entitle it
to be called valuable, and there is not in the case of Helen.
This is a view antagonistic to that of Troilus.

We cannot here discuss this crucial debate with anything
like the fullness which is desirable. Suffice it to say here that
the opposing points of view are clear—reason (Hector, Helenus)
versus honour (Troilus, Paris). (We have found the same
antithesis in the Greek camp—Ulysses' reasonableness *versus*
the wrong-headed chivalric attitude spoken of at I, iii, 197 ff.)
Now, as the Trojans' debate is proceeding, Cassandra enters—
Cassandra, the prophetess, whose utterances must surely be
regarded as having a supernatural warrant. Her cries in this
place are in accordance with Hector's point of view: "Cry,
Trojans, cry!" she screams:

> Cry, Trojans, cry! practise your eyes with tears!
> Troy must not be, nor goodly Ilion stand;
> Our firebrand brother, Paris, burns us all.
> Cry, Trojans, cry! a Helen and a woe:
> Cry, cry! Troy burns, or else let Helen go.

                                                    (II, ii, 108–12)

If Helen is retained in Troy, then Troy will perish. That is
the prophecy, and we know that it is a true prophecy.
Admittedly, it may be held to be irrelevant to an interpretation

of the play that the Elizabethan audience doubtless knew the
outcome beforehand, the story being well known. But at any
rate, here is an inspired prophetess indicating that if Helen is
retained Troy will be overthrown. And notice the line "Our
firebrand brother, Paris, burns us all." Here there is a clear
implication that we are dealing with a case similar to that of
Achilles. Paris has seized Helen—Paris insists on keeping
Helen: for his own gratification Paris is prepared to pull down
the whole city. Individualism, again, to the detriment of one's
fellow-countrymen. Proceeding, we note that Cassandra's
prophecy is caught up by Hector into the argument:

> Now, youthful Troilus, do not these high strains
> Of divination in our sister work
> Some touches of remorse? or is your blood
> So madly hot that no discourse of reason,
> Nor fear of bad success in a bad cause,
> Can qualify the same?
>
> (II, ii, 113–18)

The view that Troilus has taken up is characterized by Hector
as being that of a man whose blood is madly hot—his passion
has got control over his reason. Hector regards Troilus as a
youth whose personality is disordered—reason should rule
passion; in Troilus passion rules reason: it is an inversion of
the true order of things in the microcosm. Troilus has a disordered personality. Moreover, Hector in these lines we have
just quoted accuses Troilus of not thinking of the results of
his deeds. Is not this precisely one of the errors that Achilles
and the other Greek disorder-figures have fallen into? We have
seen that they despise prudent generalship, calculation, discretion, and value only the external splendour of physical
fighting. Similarly Troilus, according to Hector, is so distempered that he will not even think of the possibility of "bad
success in a bad cause." Paris supports Troilus's position.
And he declares that even if he alone were involved against
the Greeks he would not hesitate.

> Were I alone to pass the difficulties
> And had as ample power as I have will,
> Paris should ne'er retract what he hath done,
> Nor faint in the pursuit.
>
> (II, ii, 139–42)

There is no discretion, no reason, here. And Priam condemns him outright:

> Paris, you speak
> Like one besotted on your sweet delights:
> You have the honey still, but these the gall;
> So to be valiant is no praise at all.
>
> (II, ii, 142–45)

Note the word "besotted". And note also the recurrence of the theme of the individual who does not consider the welfare of his fellows: "You have the honey still, but these the gall."

Hector continues to asperse the ideals of Troilus and Paris. "The reasons you allege," he declares,

> do more conduce
> To the hot passion of distemper'd blood
> Than to make up a free determination
> 'Twixt right and wrong.
>
> (II, ii, 168–71)

Again we have the conception of disordered personality—passion overthrowing reason.

Over against Troilus and Paris, then, in this argument, stand Hector, Priam, and Helenus, of whom doubtless Hector and Priam are the two most important. In following the discussion (sketchily) we have found the Troilus-Paris side convicted by the other side of illegitimate individualism, of having disordered personalities, of being disorder-figures: and we may see in them persons whose supreme value is *honour* which defies reason. To a large extent they resemble Hotspur in *I Henry IV*. Hector opposes them—but, remarkably, at the end of the scene he indulges in a complete *volte-face*. He suddenly announces himself as holding after all to the honour value which he has already shown to be contrary to reason. Having stated his opposition to Paris and Troilus, he says:

> Hector's opinion
> Is this in way of truth; yet ne'ertheless,
> My spritely brethren, I propend to you
> In resolution to keep Helen still,
> For 'tis a cause that hath no mean dependance
> Upon our joint and several dignities.
>
> (II, ii, 188–93)

Now how are we to interpret this *volte-face* of Hector's? Are we supposed by Shakespeare to take it that Hector has abandoned what he now regards as having been a wrong value? I cannot think so. And the very moment when Hector is going over to the side of Troilus and Paris he says that what he has previously maintained is his opinion "in way of truth"—nevertheless he is going to change his recommendation. It seems to me that Shakespeare indicates to us clearly that in recommending that Helen be retained and that the war be continued Hector is recommending a course which he really feels to be wrong. I believe that two points should be made here: (i) we are meant by Shakespeare to take the original views of Hector (supported by Priam and the prophetess Cassandra) as the sound ones, and (ii) Troilus and Paris are disorder-figures, but Hector is also a disorder-figure, for he deliberately advocates a course which he knows to be incorrect, and deliberately supports a value which he knows to be wrong. In a sense he is less defensible than Troilus or Paris, for they are blind to the truth, but he is alive to the truth and deliberately sets it aside. I believe that this view of Hector's *volte-face* is confirmed when we take the play as a whole.

Consider the manner of Hector's death. He falls a victim to dishonourable conduct of the basest kind on the part of Achilles. There is certainly a contrast here between chivalrous conduct on the part of Hector and unchivalrous conduct on the part of Achilles. Hector is a brave man, and a victim of treachery, and to that extent he calls forth our sympathy and Achilles our detestation. But the matter is not so simple as that.

Hector goes out to battle (and to his death) against advice. He goes out against the advice of Andromache, Cassandra and Priam. He goes out in the name of honour. He is warned not to go, but he declares that he has vowed to go and therefore must go. This is the attitude of the chivalric hero. The day may be an ill-fated one: nevertheless, Hector says,

> Life every man holds dear; but the brave man
> Holds honour far more precious-dear than life.
>> (V, iii, 27–8)

Sufficient has been said to indicate that I cannot agree with Mr. Wilson Knight as regards his view of the Greek-Trojan antithesis. I am more impressed by the similarity between conditions on the Greek and Trojan sides. On both sides we have a state of prevalent disorder. I take it that as regards this play Shakespeare wants us to believe in the validity of reason. On the Trojan side, characters like Troilus, Paris, and ultimately Hector himself, reject reason; Priam upholds it. On the Greek side, we have reason represented by Ulysses, but we have conspicuous symbols of unreason in characters like Ajax and Achilles. It cannot be said that the Greeks as a whole represent reason. Achilles certainly at no point represents reason.

This brings us back to the Greeks. We have spoken of Achilles in his tent, holding himself apart from the Greek military effort. He is afflicted with self-love, pride. As Ulysses says:

> imagined worth
> Holds in his blood such swoln and hot discourse
> That 'twixt his mental and his active parts
> Kingdom'd Achilles in commotion rages
> And batters down himself.
>
> (II, iii, 182-6)

Achilles' personality is like a kingdom racked and ruined by civil war. Ulysses sets out to try to purge Achilles of his humour of self-love. We may say that he nearly succeeds, but actually he does not. In III, iii, we have him arguing with Achilles. He argues that a man cannot really be said to possess this or that quality until it affects other people: according to him, a man

> Cannot make boast to have that which he hath,
> Nor feels not what he owes, but by reflection;
> As when his virtues shining upon others
> Heat them and they retort that heat again
> To the first giver.
>
> (III, iii, 98-102)

> no man is the lord of any thing,
> Though in and of him there be much consisting,
> Till he communicate his parts to others.
>
> (III, iii, 115-17)

He is assailing Achilles as excessively individualistic. (And we may remember again that at the end Hector, to satisfy his own personal honour, destroys not only himself but Troy.) Ulysses succeeds in discomposing Achilles; but he does not succeed in getting him back into co-operation with the other Greeks in the war against Troy, because Achilles has another reason for isolating himself from the combat. He is in love with a daughter of Priam. At V, i, 42 ff., we have Achilles saying:

> I am thwarted quite
> From my great purpose in tomorrow's battle.
> Here is a letter from Queen Hecuba,
> A token from her daughter, my fair love,
> Both taxing me and gaging me to keep
> An oath that I have sworn. I will not break it:
> Fall Greeks; fail fame; honour or go or stay;
> My major vow lies here, this I'll obey.

Again we are struck by the Greek-Trojan parallelism rather than by any contrast. Achilles has sworn a vow—he will keep that vow, even if it means the "fall" of his people, the Greeks. Similarly, at the end Hector has sworn a vow—he will keep it, even though he is told on supernatural authority that it will mean the destruction of his city, Troy. It is the same thing; and there is the piquant contrast—Achilles' vow prevents him from fighting, Hector's vow makes him go out to fight. In deference to an honour-value which is clearly a matter of unwarrantable personal pride each of them does his fellow-countrymen disservice.

Achilles refrains from going into battle on account of a vow made to his mistress. And when at last he does go into battle he is no less a disordered personality than he has been hitherto—he goes out in a frenzy, in a mad search for vengeance on account of the slaying of the unworthy Patroclus. At the end we have Hector as a disordered personality, and Achilles as a disordered personality. This is a play about disorder, and *the disorder is never set right.*

Now what of the love story, the story of Troilus and Cressida which gives the play its title? Cressida is surely a simple enough case. There is no reason to doubt the sincerity of her love for Troilus; but she simply has not the moral fibre

equired for fidelity. She falses Troilus, and as she does so she
uiets her feelings of discomfort by a glib and facile "justi-
cation", the shallowness of which is mirrored in the character
f the verse which she speaks at this point:

> Troilus, farewell! one eye yet looks on thee;
> But with my heart the other eye doth see.
> Ah, poor our sex! this fault in us I find,
> The error of our eye directs our mind:
> What error leads must err; O, then conclude
> Minds sway'd by eyes are full of turpitude.
>   (V, ii, 107–12)

Troilus is a more difficult matter for interpretation. Is his
ve presented as a glorious yearning for the infinite, a soaring
spiration, or is it presented in an unfavourable light? Mr.
Vilson Knight would have us take the former of these views,
rofessor Oscar J. Campbell the latter. Troilus is surely
resented critically in the war story, and we cannot be sur-
rised if this is found to accord with the way in which he is
resented in the love story. He is deeply in love, certainly:
ut is it the kind of love that Shakespeare wants us to accept
s an admirable ideal? I agree with Professor Campbell here,
ather than with Mr. Wilson Knight. It seems to me that
ght from the start Troilus's love for Cressida is presented by
hakespeare in such a way as to make us feel that it is not to
e regarded as a case of sublime aspiration but rather as
omething the reverse of sublime. Indeed we have not read
ery far in the play before we are induced, by Troilus's own
ords, to think of his love as something *unhealthy*. In Act I,
cene i, Troilus, speaking to Pandarus, says this (line 51 ff.):

>   I tell thee I am mad
> In Cressid's love: thou answer'st 'she is fair';
> Pour'st in the open ulcer of my heart
> Her eyes, her hair, her cheek, her gait, her voice, . . .

>   instead of oil and balm,
> Thou lay'st in every gash that love hath given me
> The knife that made it.

he conceit according to which the heart of the lover is
ounded is, of course, a commonplace. The lady's beauty is

often said even to kill the lover. But the turn which Shakespeare
gives to the conceit of the wounded heart here in *Troilus and
Cressida* is, it seems to me, very remarkable. His wounded
heart has *gashes* in it—a strong word—and, more significant,
his wounded heart is an *open ulcer*. This word "ulcer" cannot
make us think of anything pleasant. We think of disease,
decomposition, decay—the idea is unpleasant in the extreme.
The passage we are considering occurs very early in the play,
and this is the impression that Shakespeare gives us of Troilus's
love early in the play. Troilus's love is a disease—his heart is
festering. I cannot think that Shakespeare chose to use this
word idly, without significance. Right at the outset he takes
the trouble to present us with this conception of love as a
disease: and it is no matter of a pretty convention—the word
"ulcer" is a horrible word, and (though this is perhaps less to
be stressed) the word "gash" itself has not very pleasant
associations.

In the war story, as we have seen, Troilus appears as a
disordered personality: his love is a disorder too, a disease.
It is true that later on Troilus the lover displays a striving
after the infinite—a wish that the limitations of his finiteness
could be surmounted: "This is the monstruosity in love, lady,"
he says to Cressida, "that the will is infinite and the execution
confined, that the desire is boundless and the act a slave to
limit" (III, ii, 87 ff.). But there is no reason why we should
automatically regard a man who, a finite being, yearns after
the infinite, as a person to praise and admire for that. In love
Troilus's ideal is certainly against reason: but the question is
whether Shakespeare wishes us to accept reason as valid or
not: and the fact that so early in the play Troilus speaks of
his love-stricken heart as ulcerated seems to me significant—
Shakespeare is clearly guiding us. I think that as regards the
way in which Shakespeare wants us to conceive of Troilus's
love Professor O. J. Campbell is on the right lines and Mr
Wilson Knight on the wrong lines.

I have not the space for anything approaching a complete
interpretative account of this play. But at least I want to
emphasize that it seems to me that Shakespeare is concerned
with disorder on *both* sides, Greek and Trojan. On both sides

we have order-figures—Ulysses, Priam: but on both sides we have conspicuous disorder-figures, and the order-figures are powerless to correct them.

In this play Shakespeare is concerned with the idea of a whole world, Greek and Trojan together, in which disorder prevails and in which the disorder does not, cannot, give way to order in the end. Order-figures like Ulysses and Priam cannot prevail against the disorder—it is too strong for them: and the disorder-figures remain disorder-figures to the end. Thus when Achilles finally does enter the fight again, it is not because right values have prevailed with him—he goes into the fight in a frenzy in order to revenge the death of Patroclus. Hector goes into the fight at the end in obedience to values which are shown by Shakespeare to be wrong. Cressida is unfaithful to Troilus, and we have no repentance, no punishment—she simply appears at the end as the type of female infidelity and we are left with the imaginative impression of her going on to the end of time as that and that only. Troilus, having been disillusioned, rushes into battle and does "mad and fantastic execution" upon the Greeks (V, v, 38)—note these words, "mad and fantastic." The play ends with disorder still triumphant, most unusually for Shakespeare. Thersites illuminates for us not only the Greek world but the world of the play as a whole.

I have spoken of my admiration of some of Mr. Wilson Knight's criticism: but in the case of this play I am convinced that he is quite wrong. I would recommend my readers, if they wish to study *Troilus and Cressida* closely, to read at any rate two works which deal with it much more satisfactorily in my view than Mr. Wilson Knight does—namely, Miss Ellis-Fermor's brilliant essay on it in her book, *The Frontiers of Drama* (1945), and Professor Campbell's book, *Comicall Satyre and Shakespeare's "Troilus and Cressida"* (1938). The reader will find differences between these two works, but he will find both of them highly illuminating: I have done so, and must acknowledge a considerable debt to both of them.

Professor Campbell holds that *Troilus and Cressida* is an essay in a dramatic genre—"comical satire"—invented by Ben

Jonson. Jonson described by that name three of his plays, the first being *Every Man Out of his Humour* (1599). Professor Campbell's theory is highly interesting. I do not propose to discuss it here, because one would find oneself in the midst of thorny problems such as, for example, the date of *Troilus and Cressida*: but I recommend the reader of this book to study Professor Campbell's work. Professor Campbell also has an essay on the play in his book, *Shakespeare's Satire* (1943).

CHAPTER V

HISTORY

In the history plays Shakespeare deals with the conceptions of order and disorder with particular reference to the body politic. These plays should be considered in the light of the views held by various of his contemporaries concerning the nature and function of history in general, and concerning the significance of the actual previous history of their own country. We cannot deal with this in detail, and the reader is referred to two recent books of importance—Dr. E. M. W. Tillyard's *Shakespeare's History Plays*, published in 1944, and Professor Lily B. Campbell's *Shakespeare's "Histories,"* published in 1947.

When he wrote his various history plays Shakespeare was not interested merely in chronicling events that had taken place in the past. He was doing that, of course; but his view of history (and it was not peculiar to him) was that past events have a vital significance for the present and the future. Look into past history, and you will find valuable lessons for present and future. Study past history, and you will see God's providence working in the world of men as it always works and always will.

With the exception of *King John*, all the Shakespeare plays called "Histories" in the first folio concern the period extending from the reign of Richard II to that of Henry VIII. The great English chronicler, Edward Hall, saw this stretch of history as embodying a connected pattern, and Dr. Tillyard has shown how Shakespeare has a similar conception of pattern.

This stretch of history was of peculiar interest to Shakespeare's contemporaries. The marriage of Henry VII to the Lady Elizabeth of York united the houses of Lancaster and

York between which there had been such bitter strife. As
Hall wrote, "the old divided controversy between the . . .
families of Lancaster and York, by the union of matrimony
celebrate and consummate between the high and mighty
prince King Henry the Seventh and the lady Elizabeth, his
most worthy Queen, the one being indubitate heir of the
house of Lancaster, and the other of York, was suspended
. . . in the person of their most noble, puissant and mighty
heir King Henry the Eighth, and by him clearly buried and
perpetually extinct."[1] Apparently, then, living under the rule
of Henry VIII's daughter Elizabeth, Shakespeare's contemporaries might be regarded as having reason to feel a sense
of security. At any rate, as Tout says, the marriage of Henry
VII made it certain "that the children of Henry and Elizabeth
would have a clearer title to the throne than any king after
Richard II."

Nevertheless, Shakespeare's contemporaries, in the last
decade of the sixteenth century, were afflicted by a sense of
insecurity and fear. What would happen when Elizabeth
should die? She refused to indicate an heir—doubtless afraid
that, if she did, her subjects, or some of them, would transfer
their allegiance prematurely. And as it became clear that she
was declining, many feared that after her death there would
be a recurrence of civil strife. The former civil strife was called
to mind with dread. And that strife, which had been finally
settled by the marriage of Henry VII—how had it originated?
It had ultimately originated with the deposition of Richard II
by Henry IV. Hall on his title-page speaks of his chronicle as
dealing with "the union of the two noble . . . families of
Lancaster and York, being long in continual dissension for
the crown of this noble realm, with all the acts done in . . .
the times of the princes, both of the one lineage and of the
other, beginning at the time of King Henry the Fourth, the
first author of this division, and so successively proceeding to
the reign of the high and prudent prince King Henry the
Eighth, the indubitate flower and very heir of both the said
lineages."[2]

[1] In this quotation, spelling and punctuation have been modernized.
[2] Spelling and punctuation have been modernized.

Fear of a recurrence of such civil warfare was a very real thing in the 1590's. The peaceful accession of James I in 1603 came as a surprise to many. Dr. G. B. Harrison quotes the diary of Lady Anne Clifford: "About 10 o'clock King *James* was proclaimed in *Cheapside* by all the Council with great joy and triumph. I went to see and hear. This peaceable coming in of the King was unexpected by all sorts of people."[1] And here is the testimony of Samuel Daniel. He wrote a poem in eight books—the "Civil Wars between the two Houses of York and Lancaster", the first four books of which were published in 1595, the year of the composition of Shakespeare's *Richard II* (Shakespeare made use of them): the complete poem was published in 1609. In the dedicatory epistle in 1609 Daniel speaks of the work as having been first undertaken "in a time which was not so well secur'd of the future, as God be blessed now it is."

When Shakespeare wrote *Richard II*, then, he and his contemporaries were faced with an uncertain future in which civil war seemed not unlikely. These fears existed, indeed, even earlier than 1595. We may say that all of Shakespeare's history plays (except *Henry VIII*, which belongs to the very end of his career as a dramatist) were written at a time of uncertainty and fear for the future. Again and again, we may say, he is giving warning to his times—here is what civil war is like: here is how it is brought about: here is a picture of the horrors it involves: here are things which in the future must be avoided at all costs.

We have spoken of how Hall sees the progression of history from Richard II to Henry VIII as a single pattern. He treats it as such in his chronicle. Shakespeare does not handle all that material as a single design. He splits it up. At the beginning of his career we have the *Henry VI* and *Richard III* plays (approx. 1590–1593): then, after an interval, he goes back and gives us a second series dealing with material earlier than that of the first set—*Richard II* belongs to 1595, the *Henry IV* plays to 1597–8, *Henry V* to 1599. *Henry VIII* belongs to

---

[1] Quoted by Dr. Harrison in the course (p. 54) of a valuable essay on Elizabethan Melancholy appended to his edition (1929) of Nicholas Breton's *Melancholike Humours*.

1612 or so. But there is no doubt that Shakespeare saw history in the same light as Hall saw it. Dr. Tillyard shows that. Shakespeare splits the big design up into—essentially—two sections: each section he handles in four plays. I propose in this chapter to deal only with the great second tetralogy—*Richard II, I and II Henry IV, and Henry V*. For we have not the space to discuss all the plays, and this second tetralogy probably represents Shakespeare's greatest achievement in the field of historical drama.[1]

The Richard II, Henry IV, and Henry V plays together constitute a single dramatic design. Dr. Johnson pointed this out: "*Shakespeare* has apparently designed a regular connection of these dramatick histories from *Richard the second* to *Henry the fifth*."[2] This is true. When Shakespeare wrote *Richard II* he doubtless had the intention of proceeding right up to *Henry V*. It is true that the plays are not all stylistically homogeneous. They were not composed in uninterrupted sequence. The two parts of *Henry IV* were. But, according to Sir Edmund Chambers's chronology, three plays intervened between the composition of *Richard II* and that of *Henry IV*, and one play between the composition of *Henry IV* and *Henry V*.[3] Yet Shakespeare takes care to connect them all up; the end of *Richard II*, for example, is both an end and a beginning. They embody indeed a single great dramatic plan.

What is the connecting thread? We begin with a bad king —we end with the ideal king. Throughout the trilogy Shakespeare is fundamentally concerned with the question, what is the nature of the ideal king? To the Elizabethan mind a good king was quintessentially necessary to order in the body politic. In the trilogy Shakespeare begins with a state of great disorder in the body politic, the disorder being laid to the charge of a bad king. An attempt to cure this disorder by means which are themselves disorderly brings about further disorder. And at last order is produced when a good king

[1] In this case the term trilogy is actually more appropriate than tetralogy, since *I and II Henry IV* constitute a single play—a mighty play, the great scope and length of which necessitated division into two parts. See the introduction to Professor Dover Wilson's edition of *I Henry IV* (1946).
[2] See W. Raleigh, *Johnson on Shakespeare* (1931 edition), p. 113.
[3] See Chambers, *William Shakespeare* (1930) Vol. I, pp. 270-1.

ascends the throne, that good king being himself a regenerated disorder-figure. The process of his regeneration is a vital part of the total design. But let us trace out the total design in fuller detail, beginning with the play of *Richard II*.

.   .   .   .   .

Richard II is king by right of succession, and he *looks* every inch a king—he *looks* like what a king should look like. The king is the supreme being in the body politic. The sun is supreme among the planets: the eagle is supreme among the birds: and so, according to the doctrine of correspondences, the king may be compared to the sun and to the eagle. These are symbols of true royalty. And in the play people look at Richard and think of the sun and of the eagle. His external aspect is truly royal. As Richard appears on the walls of Flint Castle, Bolingbroke exclaims:

> See, see, King Richard doth himself appear,
> As doth the blushing discontented sun
> From out the fiery portal of the east,
> When he perceives the envious clouds are bent
> To dim his glory and to stain the track
> Of his bright passage to the occident.

(The envious clouds represent the rebellious nobles, his enemies, Bolingbroke himself being one of them.) And the Duke of York declares:

> Yet looks he like a king: behold, his eye,
> As bright as is the eagle's, lightens forth
> Controlling majesty: . . . .
>
> (III, iii, 62-70)

But here we have a case of that favourite Shakespearian theme, the discrepancy between appearance and reality. Richard looks like a true king; but actually he is a very bad king. He is giddy, wasteful, susceptible to flattery. He likes

> Lascivious metres, to whose venom sound
> The open ear of youth doth always listen; . . . .
>
> (II, i, 19-20)

He is addicted to vanity and folly. His life is a "rash fierce blaze of riot" (II, i, 33). He recklessly spends "that which his

triumphant father's hand had won" (II, i, 181). He wastes
his wealth and is untrue to his valiant ancestors:

> Wars have not wasted it, for warr'd he hath not,
> But basely yielded upon compromise
> That which his noble ancestors achieved with blows:
> More hath he spent in peace than they in wars.
>
> (II, i, 252–5)

(The reference is to the cession of Brest to the Duke of Brit-
tany.) Richard abuses England with financial exactions which
he then squanders.

Richard produces disorder in his kingdom because he is
himself a microcosm in which disorder flourishes. In him, as
York says, "will doth mutiny with wit's regard" (II, 1, 28).
"Regard" means "thoughtful attention, consideration," and
the "wit" is the understanding. According to the hierarchical
picture of the universe, the highest part of the human brain
consisted of two parts, the understanding and the will. The
will is that faculty which decides a man to do one thing rather
than another. It is the will which chooses the course of action
that the man pursues. Man's will is free. He can do anything
he likes. But in the correctly ordered personality the will
accepts the recommendations of the understanding. In Richard
it is not so. In him the will rebels against the understanding.
It is with him as with Adam and Eve after the Fall: in them,
as Milton tells us,

> Understanding rul'd not, and the Will
> Heard not her lore.[1]

In Richard's "little state of man" there is civil war: order is
upset: "degree is shaked". His will chooses the wrong course
of conduct for him, in defiance of his understanding, and in
his conduct as king he goes against the principle of degree.
As king he should maintain order: he actually produces
disorder in the kingdom.

A particularly significant instance of disorder produced by
Richard springs from his seizure, after John of Gaunt's death,
of the latter's property, his "plate, coin, revenues and move-
ables"—that is, the legitimate inheritance of the banished

[1] See Tillyard, *Elizabethan World Picture*, p. 69.

Bolingbroke. This act is contrary to the law of order, and the
Duke of York shows that by committing it Richard is under-
mining his own position as king—virtually deposing himself.
Bolingbroke is entitled to his father's possessions by the laws
of succession; Richard is entitled to his throne by these same
laws. If Richard denies Bolingbroke the possessions of his
father, he is renouncing the laws of succession—that is, he is
renouncing the basis of his own position as king. He is, to
repeat, virtually deposing himself. To deny the laws of succession is, moreover, unnatural. It is like denying that tomorrow
will follow today—it is upsetting the universal order. York
says to him:

> Seek you to seize and gripe into your hands
> The royalties and rights of banish'd Hereford? . . . .
> Take Hereford's rights away, and take from Time
> His charters and his customary rights;
> Let not to-morrow then ensue to-day;
> Be not thyself; for how art thou a king
> But by fair sequence and succession?
>
> (II, i, 189–99)

To deny the right of tomorrow to succeed today is to disrupt
the whole order of the universe. That is what Richard is doing,
in addition to virtually deposing himself.

Nor does this exhaust the sum of Richard's sins against the
principle of order. He has been guilty of the blood of his
uncle, the Duke of Gloucester, murdered on his orders. Again
Richard has committed an unnatural deed, a deed against the
principle of order.

Altogether, then, Richard, who should maintain order in
the kingdom, actually causes disorder in it, by deeds of commission and of omission. This reversal is emphasized throughout the play. And it is, as we have seen, a direct result of
Richard's being himself a disordered personality.

.   .   .   .   .

Throughout the play of *Richard II* there is expressed again
and again a passionate love of England—an intense desire for
her welfare, a deep concern for her misfortunes, a glowing
pride in "this blessed plot, this earth, this realm, this England."

And in the play England is placed in a terrible dilemma
Richard is a bad king, under whom the country is being
ruined. On the other hand, the act of getting rid of him by
force is presented unequivocally as an act of sacrilege, a
heinous crime against that same law of order that Richard
himself had so grievously offended against.

According to the assumptions made in the play, Richard is
right in speaking of his "sacred blood". The Lord is on the
side of His anointed. "Not all the water in the rough rude
sea," says Richard,

> Can wash the balm off from an anointed king;
> The breath of wordly men cannot depose
> The deputy elected by the Lord:
> For every man that Bolingbroke hath press'd
> To lift shrewd steel against our golden crown,
> God for his Richard hath in heavenly pay
> A glorious angel: then, if angels fight,
> Weak men must fall, for heaven still guards the right.
>
> (III, ii, 54–62)

It would, of course, be a gross error to take this talk of Richard's
as in any way partaking of the nature of hybris: it is the orthodox
thought of Shakespeare's age. It is echoed by other characters
in the play—characters the portrayal of which must make us
respect them and their views. Gloucester's widow urges John
of Gaunt to exact vengeance for her husband's death. She
says:

> Edward's seven sons, whereof thyself art one,
> Were as seven vials of his sacred blood,
> Or seven fair branches springing from one root:
> Some of those seven are dried by nature's course,
> Some of those branches by the Destinies cut;
> But Thomas, my dear lord, my life, my Gloucester,
> One vial full of Edward's sacred blood,
> One flourishing branch of his most royal root,
> Is crack'd, and all the precious liquor spilt,
> Is hack'd down, and his summer leaves all faded,
> By envy's hand and murder's bloody axe.
>
> (I, ii, 11–21)

She wants vengeance: her grief cries aloud for satisfaction.

She also puts a prudential consideration before Gaunt—he
may be the next victim:

> to safeguard thine own life,
> The best way is to venge my Gloucester's death.
>
> (I, ii, 35–6)

But Gaunt cannot raise his hand against his king: Heaven will
avenge the deed when Heaven sees fit to do so. God's is the
quarrel, says Gaunt,

> for God's substitute,
> His deputy anointed in His sight,
> Hath caused his death: the which if wrongfully,
> Let heaven revenge; for I may never lift
> An angry arm against His minister.
>
> (I, ii, 37–41)

I have spoken of England being placed in a dilemma.
Under Richard the kingdom is being ruined: to proceed
violently against Richard would be a heinous crime: what is
England to do? Gaunt has the true answer according to the
principle of order—England must wait for God to act. What
actually happens is that Richard is deposed by Bolingbroke
and his supporters. And that that is presented as a crime there
can be no possible doubt.

In connection with the rebellion against Richard and in
connection with his deposition, the play is full of prophecies
of future agonies for England. Richard himself prophesies these
agonies. We have already quoted Richard as saying that God
has an army of angels to fight on his, Richard's, side (III, ii,
58 ff.). A little later on he reverts to this theme: he says to
Northumberland, one of the principal rebels, that

> God omnipotent,
> Is mustering in his clouds on our behalf
> Armies of pestilence; and they shall strike
> Your children yet unborn and unbegot,
> That lift your vassal hands against my head
> And threat the glory of my precious crown.
> Tell Bolingbroke—for yond methinks he stands—
> That every stride he makes upon my land
> Is dangerous treason: he is come to open
> The purple testament of bleeding war;
> But ere the crown he looks for live in peace,

> Ten thousand bloody crowns of mothers' sons
> Shall ill become the flower of England's face,
> Change the complexion of her maid-pale peace
> To scarlet indignation and bedew
> Her pastures' grass with faithful English blood.
>
> (III, iii, 85–100)

Bolingbroke's insurrection will result in civil war—the deaths of thousands of innocent people—discord, chaos, pestilence—a long futurity of misery: and this is the vengeance of God for the wrong done to Him in the attack on His representative. In the sequel play we see Richard's prophecy fulfilled: it is a true prophecy. And Richard is not the only prophet. The Bishop of Carlisle later takes up the theme. "What subject can give sentence on his king?" he asks (IV, i, 121). Richard is "the figure of God's majesty, His captain, steward, deputy-elect"; Bolingbroke is a traitor to his king; and, Carlisle goes on, if Bolingbroke is invested with Richard's crown, if Richard is deposed and replaced by an usurper,

> let me prophesy:
> The blood of English shall manure the ground,
> And future ages groan for this foul act;
> Peace shall go sleep with Turks and infidels,
> And in this seat of peace tumultuous wars
> Shall kin with kin and kind with kind confound;
> Disorder, horror, fear and mutiny
> Shall here inhabit, and this land be call'd
> The field of Golgotha and dead men's skulls.
> O, if you raise this house against this house,
> It will the woefullest division prove
> That ever fell upon this cursed earth.
>
> (IV, i, 136–47)

The penalty of this act of usurpation will be age upon age of "disorder, horror, fear and mutiny." This note is sounded repeatedly in the play. The play keeps pointing forward. Speaking to the rebel Northumberland, Richard says that after the usurpation the rebels will soon disagree with each other: cupidity on the part of the new king's supporters, and mistrust of them by him, will produce new disorder out of this illegitimate attempt to establish order. Richard addresses Northumberland:

> Northumberland, thou ladder wherewithal
> The mounting Bolingbroke ascends my throne,
> The time shall not be many hours of age
> More than it is ere foul sin gathering head
> Shall break into corruption: thou shalt think,
> Though he divide the realm and give thee half,
> It is too little, helping him to all;
> And he shall think that thou, which know'st the way
> To plant unrightful kings, wilt know again,
> Being ne'er so little urged, another way
> To pluck him headlong from the usurped throne.
>
> (V, i, 55–65)

Again, it is a true prophecy: in the sequel play we see this disagreement come about. The end of *Richard II* is, as we have said, both a conclusion and a beginning. The usurper has to bear a heavy load of guilt, and not he alone, but the whole of England, has to suffer for it.

To regard the deposition of Richard as a sin does not mean that one should blind oneself in the slightest degree to his deficiencies as king. We must always keep the correct balance between the two factors. John of Gaunt refuses to proceed violently against Richard over Gloucester's death because Richard is God's anointed: but this same John of Gaunt fearlessly reproves Richard for his unkingly ways. And the Duke of York is in the same position. He knows Richard for what he is: he knows that the evils of the time are a result of Richard's conduct, that this is "the sick hour that his surfeit made" (II, ii, 84). But he knows also that to rebel against Richard is to rebel against God's appointed representative. "My lords of England," he says,

> let me tell you this:
> I have had feeling of my cousin's wrongs
> And labour'd all I could to do him right;
> But in this kind to come, in braving arms,
> Be his own carver and cut out his way,
> To find out right with wrong, it may not be;
> And you that do abet him in this kind
> Cherish rebellion and are rebels all.
>
> (II, iii, 140–47)

Bolingbroke has legitimate grievances—York allows that. But

this is the wrong way to right them: the fact that the grievances
exist is no condonation of the methods Bolingbroke is using
to rectify them.

.   .   .   .   .

The deposition of Richard, then, is presented as a heinous
crime. In the deposition scene (IV, i) Richard accuses the
rebels of their sin, and he goes so far as to compare them with
Pilate, himself with Christ. He is in an even worse case than
Christ was: of his oppressors he says:

> Did they not sometime cry, 'all hail!' to me?
> So Judas did to Christ: but he, in twelve,
> Found truth in all but one; I, in twelve thousand, none.
>
> (IV, i, 169–71)

In comparing them to Pilate and Judas, and himself to Christ,
Richard is not blaspheming. To the Elizabethan mind the
comparison would appear perfectly legitimate, and it emphasizes the seriousness of the matter.

This deposition scene is a most remarkable and crucial
one, and will bear further examination. In his edition of the
play, Professor Dover Wilson has done us a service by re-
minding us of Walter Pater's treatment of the play in his
Appreciations, in the essay entitled "Shakespeare's English
Kings". Pater suggests that the deposition scene is a piece of
ritual—an *inversion* of the coronation service. A king becomes
a subject (Richard), a subject becomes a king (Bolingbroke);
and this inversion is given powerful imaginative reinforcement
by the fact that the deposition scene is conceived as an inverted
coronation rite. The outward trappings of royalty are taken
off solemnly, one by one. Richard does it himself—for he
willingly submits to deposition: the scene is a deposition scene
and at the same time an abdication scene. Note the ritualistic
tone with which Richard divests himself of the marks of
royalty:

> With mine own tears I wash away my balm,
> With mine own hands I give away my crown,
> With mine own tongue deny my sacred state,
> With mine own breath release all duty's rites: . . .
>
> (IV, i, 207–10)

nd so on. It is a very solemn moment: and it is a great sin
at is being committed.

Now in the course of this scene Richard develops an
genious idea. If to depose a king is a crime against God's
w, then not only Northumberland, Bolingbroke, and the
hers, are guilty of that sin, but Richard himself also—by
nsenting to give up his throne he is himself deposing a king:

> Mine eyes are full of tears, I cannot see:
> And yet salt water blinds them not so much
> But they can see a sort of traitors here.
> Nay, if I turn mine eyes upon myself,
> I find myself a traitor with the rest;
> For I have given here my soul's consent
> To undeck the pompous body of a king;
> Made glory base and sovereignty a slave,
> Proud majesty a subject, state a peasant.
>
> (IV, i, 244–52)

he sin consists in violently inverting a relationship which is
tablished by the law of order. Northumberland, Bolingbroke,
d the rest, are guilty of this sin against order: Richard
ggests that he himself is similarly guilty here.

Now this may legitimately be called an ingenious, a clever,
lea. Richard displays this sort of ingenuity elsewhere in the
ene also. At one point Bolingbroke calls Richard "fair
usin". And Richard retorts:

> 'Fair cousin'? I am greater than a king:
> For when I was a king, my flatterers
> Were then but subjects; being now a subject,
> I have a king here to my flatterer.
> Being so great, I have no need to beg.
>
> (IV, i, 305–9)

his sort of ingenious juggling with ideas is highly charac-
ristic of Richard. He cleverly plays with the inversion idea.

There is perhaps no instance *more* striking than this scene
f how Shakespeare can endow the same thing with more than
e kind of significance. Richard's behaviour in this scene,
cluding his accusation of himself as guilty of the crime of
eposing a king, indicates imaginative virtuosity. It would not be
nfair to say that in this scene—and indeed throughout the

play—Richard appears to be an artistic type. Indeed, part of
his unkingliness comes from his being an artist. He is an artist
miscast as king. He is not a heroic type, nor is he distinguished
by any political intelligence. This aspect of him is admirably
expounded by Sir Edmund Chambers in his *Shakespeare: A
Survey* (a book which is most warmly recommended to the
reader). His sending for the mirror is again the act of a kind
of artist—at any rate Richard likes to dramatize himself; he
is an actor.

His accusation of himself as guilty of deposing a king—
sin against order—suggests a man endowed with imaginative
and intellectual virtuosity. But there is another, deeper
significance. The deposition of Richard being a grievous
crime, the sympathies of the audience will inevitably be with
him. And so it should be—but not too much, since he is the
initial disorder-figure. I believe that in the deposition scene
Shakespeare is anxious that the audience should not
sympathize with Richard *too much*—should not sympathize
with him to the extent of upsetting the moral balance of the
play. I believe that when he makes Richard accuse himself
of sin in deposing a king Shakespeare intends us to cast our
minds back and remember passages earlier in the play in which
grossly unkingly conduct of Richard's has been presented as
virtual self-deposition. We remember that Richard had con-
fiscated Bolingbroke's inheritance; and we remember that the
Duke of York had suggested to Richard that that deed
involved the denial of tomorrow's right to follow today, and
also involved self-deposition on Richard's part, since he was
denying Bolingbroke the right of inheritance, which is precisely
the right by which Richard himself is king.

> Take Hereford's rights away, and take from Time
> His charters and his customary rights;
> Let not to-morrow then ensue to-day;
> Be not thyself; for how art thou a king
> But by fair sequence and succession?
>
> (II, i, 195–99)

In the deposition scene, since a crime against Richard is being
enacted, the audience's sympathies will be with him, and
rightly. But Richard has been a thoroughly bad king—he has

been initially responsible for the disorder in the kingdom—
and the audience must not be allowed to forget that. And so
Shakespeare makes Richard accuse himself of sin in the
deposition scene—the sin of deposing a king: and we remember
another sense in which earlier he had deposed a king. He
had done so by behaving in a thoroughly unkingly fashion.
Thus the audience can view the deposition scene properly:
a crime is committed against Richard, but on the other hand,
at the same time, Richard was himself a guilty man. The
crime is committed against the law of order: and Richard
himself had offended against that same law. We are made to
remember that. I should say that Shakespeare manages things
so that the audience sympathizes with Richard in the
deposition scene only to the extent which is right and proper
—to that extent, certainly, but to no greater an extent.

To get the moral balance right, we might perhaps compare
the case of Adam in connection with the Fall. Adam was
guilty of sin: his sin was, ultimately, a consequence of Satan's
sin: in contemplating Adam's sin we must not forget Satan's
original responsibility: yet at the same time we must allow
that Adam did sin. In the same sense, the sin of Bolingbroke
may be regarded as consequential on Richard's sin: that,
however, does not lessen Bolingbroke's sin: nor must we on the
other hand forget the initial sin. We must keep the balance right.
And Shakespeare skilfully helps us to do so.

.   .   .   .   .   .

Deposed and in captivity Richard comes to realize exactly
what he has been. He hears music, and he moralizes thus:

> how sour sweet music is,
> When time is broke and no proportion kept!
> So is it in the music of men's lives.
> And here have I the daintiness of ear
> To check time broke in a disorder'd string;
> But for the concord of my state and time
> Had not an ear to hear my true time broke.
> I wasted time, and now doth time waste me.
>
> (V, v, 42–9)

We have seen how Mr. Wilson Knight has shown that in

I

Shakespeare disorder is frequently thought of figuratively as music out of tune:

> Take but degree away, untune that string,
> And, hark, what discord follows!
>
> (*Troilus and Cressida*, I, iii, 109–10)

In the time of his kingship, before rebellion came against him Richard did not realize that the music of his life was being played out of tune—that he was a disordered personality. and that in his conduct he was destroying degree in the kingdom. But now he realizes it. Misfortune brings self-knowledge to him, as also, for example, to King Lear.

The manner of Richard's death arouses our sympathy for him: at the same time we cannot forget that he was ultimately responsible for all the trouble that afflicts England in this play and in the sequel plays. *Ultimately* responsible—for, as we have said, this does not lessen Bolingbroke's guilt. Bolingbroke knows himself—he knows his guilt for what it is. Though he has become king in the hope of producing order, the play ends on a note of fear of future disorder. And on a note of guilt. Bolingbroke's conscience is active within him. He desired the murder of Richard, but its accomplishment brings him, not peace of mind, but a burning sense of guilt. "Though I did wish him dead," he says (V, vi, 39), "I hate the murderer, love him murdered." And he resolves on

> a voyage to the Holy Land,
> To wash this blood off from my guilty hand.
>
> (V, vi, 49–50)

He is never able to make the journey because of troubles and disorders at home. He is never able to expiate his guilt. His becoming king was a crime, and the prophecies of Richard and the Bishop of Carlisle are fulfilled—we see them fulfilled in the *Henry IV* plays. Henry has to contend with rebellion. There is civil war still: "the blood of English doth manure the ground." The Henry IV that we meet at the beginning of the first part of his play is "shaken", "wan with care". The keynote is Nemesis.

Before we reach the end of *Richard II* we are pointed forward to the chaos of future civil war. We are also pointed forward in another important particular. Not the least of Henry IV's troubles is the character and behaviour of his son. Towards the end of *Richard II*, Bolingbroke, now King Henry IV, speaks of him, and of how he daily frequents taverns with dissolute companions:

> Even such, they say, as stand in narrow lanes,
> And beat our watch, and rob our passengers.
>
> (V, iii, 8–9)

The prince is "wanton and effeminate", "unthrifty".

> Can no man tell me of my unthrifty son?
> 'Tis full three months since I did see him last:
> If any plague hang over us, 'tis he.
>
> (V, iii, 1–3)

Now this last line carries our minds back to Richard's prophecy at III, iii, 85–90:

> Yet know, my master, God omnipotent,
> Is mustering in his clouds on our behalf
> Armies of pestilence; and they shall strike
> Your children yet unborn and unbegot,
> That lift your vassal hands against my head
> And threat the glory of my precious crown.

Henry regards his son as a *plague* hanging over him: Richard has spoken of God mustering against his, Richard's, enemies "armies of *pestilence*". Richard was not thinking of Prince Hal; but by the phraseological resemblance ("plague/pestilence") Shakespeare contrives to suggest to our minds that the young Henry's disorderliness is a part of Heaven's vengeance on Bolingbroke for his guilt. The mention of young Henry, Prince Hal, could not but suggest to the audience the thought, this will be Bolingbroke's successor." Bolingbroke supplanted Richard (paradoxically) in the name of order: Bolingbroke's successor looks as if he would be like Richard—a disorder-figure. Is this to be Bolingbroke's punishment for his crime?— he committed a sin against the law of order in an attempt to bring about order in England, but, after all his strivings, his son will be a king of the kind that Richard was? Prince Hal

is "as dissolute as desperate"; he is a representative of disorde
and that (Shakespeare *suggests* to us) is part of Bolingbroke
punishment. True, Bolingbroke sees in him

> sparks of better hope, which elder years
> May happily bring forth.
>
> (V, iii, 21-2)

At the end of *Richard II*, Shakespeare suggests the whol
course of the trilogy. But against Bolingbroke's hope of th
Prince's reformation stands the fact (far more painful than th
hope is strong) that the Prince is a libertine, a conspicuo
disorder-figure. At the end of *Richard II* we are left with th
picture of the future: the usurpation is a crime—Englan
will suffer for it—the usurper will suffer for it—the usurpe
is oppressed by a deep-seated and terribly real sense of guilt—
and his son's character and behaviour are presented to ou
imaginations as part of the usurper's punishment. All this
the case, despite the fact that in the deposition scene Richard
willingness to resign had been stressed, and Northumberlan
had stressed that Richard was worthily deposed.

.   .   .   .   .   .

And so we come to the great two-part *Henry IV* play
Heywood wrote a play the sub-title of which was *The Troubl
of Queen Elizabeth, Part I*. I suppose that it would not b
unfair to say that Shakespeare's *Henry IV* might be appro
priately sub-titled *The Troubles of Bolingbroke*. We have see
that he is to be regarded as a guilty man—he regards himsel
as that: and in this play that bears his name he is dogged b
Nemesis. The prophecies of woe uttered in *Richard II* ar
here fulfilled. Thus Richard himself had prophesied tha
Northumberland, the "ladder" by which Bolingbroke mounte
his, Richard's, throne, would come to feel that Bolingbrok
was ungrateful, had rewarded him insufficiently for his help
The prophecy is fulfilled. Henry IV has to contend wit
rebellion on the part of the Northumberland family. And tha
family does in good sooth bring forth the charge of ingratitude
Hotspur, Northumberland's son, speaks of "this unthankfu
king . . . this ingrate and canker'd Bolingbroke", and agai
of "this forgetful man" (I, iii, 136-7, 161, in Part I). H

djures his father, and his uncle Worcester, not to be "fool'd,
iscarded and shook off" by Bolingbroke (I, iii, 178). Worcester
eclares that

> bear ourselves as even as we can,
> The king will always think him in our debt,
> And think we think ourselves unsatisfied,
> Till he hath found a time to pay us home.
>
> (*I Henry IV*, I, iii, 285-8)

Richard had foreseen what would happen: it does happen.
Having read *Richard II* we cannot but regard the Northumberland rebellion against Henry IV as a nemesis. The rebels can,
of course, argue—and they do—that Henry has no just claim
to the throne. They had helped him to it, but they can—and
they do—whether sincerely or not—profess remorse for this.
They are angered by Henry's treatment of Mortimer; and
Worcester is able to say of Mortimer:

> was he not proclaim'd
> By Richard that dead is the next of blood?
>
> (*I Henry IV*, I, iii, 145-6)

Northumberland corroborates him:

> He was; I heard the proclamation:
> And then it was when the unhappy king,—
> Whose wrongs in us God pardon!—did set forth
> Upon his Irish expedition.
>
> (*I Henry IV*, I, iii, 147-50)

Worcester adds that for Richard's death the conspirators

> in the world's wide mouth.
> Live scandalized and foully spoken of.
>
> (*I Henry IV*, I, iii, 153-4)

And Hotspur enlarges on the shame of it:

> That men of your nobility and power
> Did gage them both in an unjust behalf,
> As both of you—God pardon it!—have done,
> To put down Richard, that sweet lovely rose,
> And plant this thorn, this canker, Bolingbroke.
>
> (*I Henry IV*, I, iii, 172-6)

They may not be sincere in this—they may be seizing on
excuses: but it is part of the nemesis that pursues Henry that

they can, of course, urge the illegitimacy of his succession and, at least, profess to be remorseful for their part in securing it. The rebels urge not only the illegitimacy of Henry's succession, but also the claim that he is an overbearing and unjust king. For instance, Hotspur claims that Henry has heavily taxed the whole state and has "broke oath on oath, committed wrong on wrong" (IV, iii, 101 in Part I). It is ironical that—whether or not their claims are just—they make use against Henry of the same kind of arguments as Henry had used against Richard.

The rebellion against Henry, then, is part of the penalty of his crime. Now Shakespeare suggests to our imaginations that the character and behaviour of Henry's son and heir is another part of that penalty. Prince Hal is riotous, dissolute, licentious, intemperate, disorderly. We have seen how, at the end of *Richard II*, Henry refers to him:

> If any plague hang over us, 'tis he.

And we have seen how this recalls Richard's claim that God was mustering "armies of pestilence" on his behalf. The idea was thus suggested that the character and behaviour of Prince Hal are a punishment inflicted by God on King Henry for his crime. This idea is again suggested in *I Henry IV*, although the King refers to it only as a possibility. Speaking to his son, Henry says:

> I know not whether God will have it so,
> For some displeasing service I have done,
> That, in his secret doom, out of my blood
> He'll breed revengement and a scourge for me;
> But thou dost in thy passages of life
> Make me believe that thou art only mark'd
> For the hot vengeance and the rod of heaven
> To punish my mistreadings.
>
> (*I Henry IV*, III, ii, 4–11)

He suggests that Prince Hal's character and behaviour *may be* a heavenly punishment for his own sins. He does not speak of it as a punishment for his act of usurpation. But we do not hear of Hal and his ways at all until after the usurpation is a fact. The usurpation is the principal sin of Henry's of which ve are conscious. And so the idea is conveyed to us that Hal s, indeed, a divine retribution for the usurpation.

For Henry IV, a usurper who has to contend with disorders in the state, it is essential, if he is to have any peace of mind at all, that he should be able to have confidence in the good kingship of his heir. But Henry is denied even this peace of mind. During his lifetime, his son's periods of repentance are impermanent. Fundamentally, Hal's disposition and conduct appear to Henry to be just like Richard's. He wishes that Hotspur, son of the rebel Northumberland, were his son instead of Hal. We can see what he is ultimately afraid of. He is afraid that when Hal becomes king he will be such a one as Richard was: and is he not afraid that Hal will be deposed by such a one as Hotspur, even as Richard was deposed by him himself? And so his efforts will all be brought to nought. He fears that the future will produce that pattern or rhythm—Hal deposed by Hostpur as Richard was by Hal's father, for similar reasons and by similar means. Speaking to Hal, Henry says:

> The skipping king, he ambled up and down
> With shallow jesters and rash bavin wits,
> Soon kindled and soon burnt; carded his state,
> Mingled his royalty with capering fools,
> Had his great name profaned with their scorns
> And gave his countenance, against his name,
> To laugh at gibing boys and stand the push
> Of every beardless vain comparative,
> Grew a companion to the common streets,
> Enfeoff'd himself to popularity;
> That, being daily swallow'd by men's eyes,
> They surfeited with honey and began
> To loathe the taste of sweetness, whereof a little
> More than a little is by much too much . . . .
> And in that very line, Harry, standest thou;
> For thou hast lost thy princely privilege
> With vile participation.
>
> (*I Henry IV*, III, ii, 60–73, 85–7)

And again:

> For all the world
> As thou art to this hour was Richard then
> When I from France set foot at Ravenspurgh,
> And even as I was then is Percy now.
>
> (Ibid. 93–6)

This last passage certainly suggests that Henry is afraid that when Hal becomes king he will be deposed by Hotspur. Again, Henry says:

> O that it could be proved
> That some night-tripping fairy had exchanged
> In cradle-clothes our children where they lay,
> And call'd mine Percy, his [Northumberland's] Plantagenet!
> Then would I have his Harry, and he mine.
>
> (*I Henry IV*, I, i, 86–90)

Suppose that this had happened!—Does Shakespeare present Hotspur as a man of a character suitable for kingship? The great two-part *Henry IV* play is on the one hand a result of what has gone before; and on the other hand it shows us the preliminary stages in the career of the man who is to become the ideal king. We have on the one hand the nemesis that dogs the usurper; and on the other hand we have at the end the emergence of the good king. During the play, Shakespeare is very much interested in the question, what is the character of the good king? Henry's imagination envisages Hotspur as king. Would Hotspur make a good king? The question cannot but occur to reader or audience.

Hotspur is a chivalric figure. He is fiery, impetuous, and imprudent where his honour is concerned. He reveals the essential nature of his ideal in his famous speech on honour:

> By heaven, methinks it were an easy leap,
> To pluck bright honour from the pale-faced moon,
> Or dive into the bottom of the deep,
> Where fathom-line could never touch the ground,
> And pluck up drowned honour by the locks;
> So he that doth redeem her thence might wear
> Without corrival all her dignities.
>
> (*I Henry IV*, I, iii, 201–7)

I have no doubt that, if we read these lines, magnificent as they are, in their context, we shall be unable to avoid the impression that Shakespeare means them to be uttered by a speaker whose delivery is impetuous in the extreme—the sentiment is meant to impress us as extravagant. If any reader should doubt this, there can at any rate be no doubt whatever about a passage like this:

> Love! I love thee not,
> I care not for thee, Kate: this is no world
> To play with mammets and to tilt with lips:
> We must have bloody noses and crack'd crowns,
> And pass them current too.
>
> (*I Henry IV*, II, iii, 93–7)

"Bloody noses". Is not this the accent of caricature? Is there not a distinct element of the absurd in Hotspur? Again: Hotspur and Glendower are quarrelling about the division of England. Hotspur wants to alter the course of the River Trent: Glendower objects: they wrangle: Glendower gives in: he says to Hotspur:

> Come, you shall have Trent turn'd.

And Hotspur, who has been obstinately sticking to his point, replies:

> I do not care: I'll give thrice so much land
> To any well-deserving friend;
> But in the way of bargain, mark ye me,
> I'll cavil on the ninth part of a hair.
>
> (*I Henry IV*, III, i, 136–40)

What can one say of such a man except that he is, as Professor Dover Wilson says, politically impossible?

Hotspur, then, represents an extravagant kind of chivalry. There is nobility in it—let there be no mistake about that. But he lacks moderation, restraint, temperateness, prudence. His personality is not balanced. He sometimes speaks in such a way as to lead us to think that Shakespeare is engaged on a caricature. But in addition Hotspur is explicitly criticized by other characters in the play. Thus, in III, i, of Part I, where

Hotspur annoys Glendower, he is rebuked for this by Mortimer and by Worcester. Worcester says:

> In faith, my lord, you are too wilful-blame;
> And since your coming hither have done enough
> To put him quite beside his patience.
> You must needs learn, lord, to amend this fault:
> Though sometimes it show greatness, courage, blood,—
> And that's the dearest grace it renders you,—
> Yet oftentimes it doth present harsh rage,
> Defect of manners, want of government,
> Pride, haughtiness, opinion and disdain:
> The least of which haunting a nobleman
> Loseth men's hearts and leaves behind a stain
> Upon the beauty of all parts besides,
> Beguiling them of commendation.
>
> (lines 177–89)

We are reminded of the "dram of evil" speech in *Hamlet*.

The Earl of Douglas represents the same conception of honour as Hotspur does, and he is similarly criticized. At the beginning of IV, iii, of Part I, Hotspur and Douglas want to fight at once: Worcester and Vernon counsel delay on prudential grounds. "You do not counsel well," says Douglas to Vernon, "You speak it out of fear and cold heart." And Vernon replies:

> Do me no slander, Douglas: by my life,
> And I dare well maintain it with my life,
> If well-respected honour bid me on,
> I hold as little counsel with weak fear
> As you, my lord, or any Scot that this day lives:
> Let it be seen to-morrow in the battle
> Which of us fears.
>
> (lines 8–14)

Vernon disapproves of insane rashness in the pursuit of honour. He stands by "well-respected honour"—honour which does not exclude prudence, consideration, discretion. He upholds moderation, balance—but does not abrogate honour by any means. We have already seen the Hotspur-Douglas impetuosity in *Troilus and Cressida*—"They tax our policy, and call it cowardice. . . ."

Hotspur and Douglas have their critics, then. We have

seen Worcester criticizing Hotspur. Another of Hotspur's
critics is Prince Hal himself. "I," he says, "am not yet of
Percy's mind, the Hotspur of the north; he that kills me some
six or seven dozen of Scots at a breakfast, washes his hands,
and says to his wife 'Fie upon this quiet life! I want work.'
'O my sweet Harry,' says she, 'how many hast thou killed
to-day?' 'Give my roan horse a drench', says he; and answers
'Some fourteen,' an hour after; 'a trifle, a trifle.'" (II, iv,
114 ff. in Part I). This is not so very much more a caricature
of Hotspur than Hotspur is himself a caricature.

And Falstaff is a critic of Hotspur's values. We have quoted
Hotspur on honour. Equally famous is Falstaff on honour.

> Honour pricks me on. Yea, but how if honour prick me off
> when I come on? how then? Can honour set to a leg? no: or an
> arm? no: or take away the grief of a wound? no. Honour hath
> no skill in surgery, then? no. What is honour? a word. What is
> in that word honour? what is that honour? air. A trim reckoning!
> Who hath it? he that died o' Wednesday. Doth he feel it? no.
> Doth he hear it? no. 'Tis insensible, then? Yea, to the dead.
> But will it not live with the living? no. Why? detraction will not
> suffer it. Therefore I'll none of it. Honour is a mere scutcheon:
> and so ends my catechism.
>
> (*I Henry IV*, V, i, 131 ff.)

Again, in the presence of the corpse of Sir Walter Blunt,
Falstaff says:

> I like not such grinning honour as Sir Walter hath: give me
> life: which if I can save, so; if not, honour comes unlooked for,
> and there's an end.
>
> (Ibid., V, iii, 62 ff.)

We are certainly not intended by Shakespeare to take Falstaff
as wholly right and Hotspur as wholly wrong. There is much
nobility in Hotspur and none in Falstaff. But Falstaff's words
serve to underline the undoubted fact that Hotspur is intemperate and unreasonable in his expression of his honour-
value.

Hotspur lacks discretion, he lacks moderation, balance,
and common sense. If he were to become king he would not
be a good king—Shakespeare surely implies that. Now we

have seen opposed to his values those of Falstaff and Prince
Hal (the latter being under Falstaff's influence). If Falstaff
and the Prince are right in so far as people like Hotspur are
open to criticism, yet Falstaff and the Prince are themselves
open to criticism, for their way of life is itself the reverse of
admirable. We have valid criticism by means of standards
which are themselves open to criticism, as Professor Knights
points out.[1]

The Falstaff way of life, shared by the Prince, is a life of
unrestrained fun and sensuous enjoyment, a life of immoderate
eating and drinking, a life in which highway robbery is an
amusing pastime, a life of immorality, of prodigality, of
licence, of riot. In his book, *The Fortunes of Falstaff* (1943),
Professor Dover Wilson brilliantly shows how Falstaff and
Prince Hal belong to the morality play tradition. He refers to
the moral interlude called *Youth*, written about 1520. He
summarizes it thus: "The little play opens with a dialogue
between Youth and Charity. The young man, heir to his
father's land, gives insolent expression to his self-confidence,
lustihood, and contempt for spiritual things. Whereupon
Charity leaves him, and he is joined by Riot, that is to say
wantonness, who presently introduces him to Pride and
Lechery. The dialogue then becomes boisterous, and continues
in that vein for some time, much no doubt to the enjoyment of
the audience. Yet, in the end, Charity reappears with Humility;
Youth repents; and the interlude terminates in the most seemly
fashion imaginable."

Professor Dover Wilson goes on to say that "no one
reading this lively playlet can have missed the resemblance
between Riot and Falstaff," and he enlarges on the parallelism.[2] Falstaff is descended from Riot, but he includes other
elements as well. As Wilson points out, "Hal associates
Falstaff in turn with the Devil of the miracle play, the Vice
of the morality, and the Riot of the interlude, when he calls
him 'that villainous abominable misleader of Youth, that old
white-bearded Satan', 'that reverend Vice, that grey Iniquity,
that father Ruffian, that Vanity in years', and 'the tutor and
the feeder of my riots'. 'Riot', again," Wilson continues, "is the

---

[1] *Determinations*, p. 128.   [2] Op. cit., p. 18.

word that comes most readily to King Henry's lips when speaking of his prodigal son's misconduct." Falstaff's literary ancestry is complex, for in addition to all the foregoing, as Wilson again points out, he "possesses a strain, and more than a strain, of the classical *miles gloriosus*."[1]

Prince Hal, then, is Youth, the prodigal son, and Falstaff is among other things Riot, the misleader of Youth.

Now Falstaff is great fun: we all enjoy him. But that does not mean that we must approve of his way of life. The life to which Riot tempts Youth is attractive: of course it is—otherwise Youth would not be tempted by it. But it is certainly evil. And we shall quite miss Shakespeare's point if we fail to see that Falstaff's way of life is evil and is presented by Shakespeare as evil. Professor Knights rightly emphasizes "the disease aspect of Falstaff".[2] Falstaff's way of life leads to bodily diseases: its ultimate consequences are disgusting. The rejection of Falstaff at the end of *II Henry IV* has troubled many critics who think that the character of Hal, now King Henry V, shows up badly as a result of the episode. He renounces his old boon companion, which is, many readers say, the act of a cad. But to think this is to make nonsense of the design of the entire trilogy. If we think of the situation in terms of the morality tradition to which it belongs we shall get it in proper focus.

Having been misled by Riot, Youth finally repents: in the end Youth makes the right choice: the prodigal son returns. And if we, the readers or audience, think of Falstaff as hardly used by Hal—if we think of Hal as an ungrateful cad—it means that we ourselves have been dazzled by the attractive aspect of the evil life by which the prodigal was tempted. It means that we have not paid sufficient attention to the disagreeable aspects of Falstaff, to the disease aspect of Falstaff. I have several times referred to Professor Knights's essay on *Henry IV*. He correctly interprets the design of the *Henry IV* plays when he says, "satire implies a standard, and in *Henry IV* the validity of the standard itself is questioned . . . 'Honour' and 'state-craft' are set in opposition to the natural life of the body, but the chief body of the play is, explicitly, 'a bolting-hutch

[1] Op. cit., p. 20.   [2] *Determinations*, p. 129.

of beastliness.'"[1] Falstaff criticizes Hotspur: Hotspur is, indeed, open to criticism: but so is Falstaff.

Falstaff is set in opposition, as Professor Knights says, not only to "honour" (Hotspur) but also to "state-craft" (Henry IV). Apart from the fact that he is a usurper, is Henry IV Shakespeare's idea of what a king should be? Does Shakespeare present Henry IV's character as thoroughly kingly?

Henry IV is a "politician" in the sense in which that word was commonly used in Elizabethan times. He believes in the use of "policy"—that is, in the use of craft, stratagems, cunning devices, in order to get what he wants. In *I Henry IV*, III, ii, Henry, reproving his son for his behaviour, explains the methods by which he himself had secured the allegiance of his supporters in Richard's time. He is not at all ashamed of these methods. He is reproaching Hal for consorting too freely with common people. He holds that it is imprudent—they are apt to get tired of one, and one loses their regard and support. So Henry argues.

> Had I so lavish of my presence been,
> So common-hackney'd in the eyes of men,
> So stale and cheap to vulgar company,
> Opinion, that did help me to the crown,
> Had still kept loyal to possession
> And left me in reputeless banishment,
> A fellow of no mark nor likelihood.
> By being seldom seen, I could not stir
> But like a comet I was wonder'd at;
> That men would tell their children 'This is he;'
> Others would say 'Where, which is Bolingbroke?'
> And then I stole all courtesy from heaven,
> And dress'd myself in such humility
> That I did pluck allegiance from men's hearts,
> Loud shouts and salutations from their mouths,
> Even in the presence of the crowned king.
>
> (lines 39–54)

These are the words of a man whose conduct has all been

---

[1] *Determinations*, pp. 128–9.

carefully calculated to conduce to the end he has in view. He
acted with courtesy and humility, not because he was essentially courteous and modest, but because he saw that it would
pay. I cannot believe that many readers of *Henry IV* can
think that Shakespeare means us to admire this altogether.
Hostpur calls Henry IV a "vile politician". We have seen that
Hotspur is characterized by an extravagant impetuosity, and
"vile" is excessive. But does Shakespeare not mean us to
regard Hotspur's criticism of Henry IV as having at least
something in it? Hotspur always speaks out with imprudent
frankness—he is the very antithesis of Henry IV. But if
Hotspur is open to criticism, so is Henry IV. We have a
veritable chain of criticism—Hotspur criticizes Henry IV;
Hotspur is himself criticized, e.g. by Falstaff; but Falstaff
is himself open to criticism, and is rightly rejected in the end.

.   .   .   .   .

At the end of *II Henry IV* we have the emergence of the
ideal king, Henry V. He reconciles himself with the Lord
Chief Justice, the representative of law and order, with whom
he had, in his unregenerate days, come into conflict. The
values of the Lord Chief Justice are the antithesis of those
of Falstaff. As king, Henry V, rejecting Falstaff, will govern
in accordance with the principles of law and order. And, as
early as the end of Part I, Hal had expressed his admiration of
Hotspur, whom he had previously satirized. He slays Hotspur
on the field at Shrewsbury; and as Hotspur lies there dead
Hal addresses him:

> fare thee well, great heart! . . .
> this earth that bears thee dead
> Bears not alive so stout a gentleman . . .
> Adieu, and take thy praise with thee to heaven!
> Thy ignominy sleep with thee in the grave,
> But not remember'd in thy epitaph!
> (*I Henry IV*, V, iv, 87, 92–3, 99–101)

It is a fair judgment. And, before the battle of Agincourt,
Hal, now Henry V, will speak in tones that remind us irresistibly

of Hotspur. Westmoreland wishes that the English at Agincourt had more men in their army. And Henry says :

> No, my fair cousin:
> If we are mark'd to die, we are enow
> To do our country loss; and if to live,
> The fewer men, the greater share of honour.
> God's will! I pray thee, wish not one man more.
> By Jove, I am not covetous for gold,
> Nor care I who doth feed upon my cost;
> It yearns me not if men my garments wear;
> Such outward things dwell not in my desires:
> But if it be a sin to covet honour,
> I am the most offending soul alive.
> No, faith, my coz, wish not a man from England:
> God's peace! I would not lose so great an honour
> As one man more, methinks, would share from me
> For the best hope I have. O, do not wish one more!
>
> (*Henry V*, IV, iii, 19–33)

These are the veritable accents of Hotspur. The difference is that Henry V's chivalry is part of the inspiration of a balanced personality. Take him all in all, and he does not appear rash, intemperate, imprudent, as Hotspur was. He may be said to exemplify the best in Hotspur, without Hotspur's faults. He speaks as in our last quotation; but he does not declare the necessity of having "bloody noses and crack'd crowns" !

Equally, he exemplifies the best in his father, but without his father's faults. Though guilty of a sin in usurping the throne, Henry IV had wanted to rule an orderly kingdom in an orderly fashion, in contrast to Richard. In Henry IV will did not mutiny with wit's regard—nor does it in his son, after his reformation. Now, as we have seen, Henry IV was a "politician"—he acted courteously, for example, because he saw that that would pay, would get him what he wanted. We have claimed that the audience is not meant to react altogether sympathetically to this. But Henry V acts according to the same principle on occasion. Thus, in the play of *Henry V*,

Bardolph is executed for robbing a church during the French campaign. And Henry says:

> We would have all such offenders so cut off: and we give express charge, that in our marches through the country, there be nothing compelled from the villages, nothing taken but paid for, none of the French upbraided or abused in disdainful language; for when lenity and cruelty play for a kingdom, the gentler gamester is the soonest winner.
>
> *(Henry V*, III, vi, 113 ff.)

The suggestion is that Henry's merciful decree is uttered mainly because the course it directs will get him what he wants. We have heard Henry V echoing the accents of Hotspur: here he seems to echo the accents of Henry IV. We have suggested that Shakespeare does not present Henry IV altogether sympathetically, on account of this sort of thing. Yet here it reappears in the man whom we are claiming as Shakespeare's picture of the ideal king. Again, the difference is that, taken as a whole, Henry V's character is more admirable than that of Henry IV. Shakespeare seems to say that "policy" is necessary in a king; but the ideal king, while using "policy" when necessary, is, nevertheless, in general characterized by a franker, a more open, a more warm-hearted disposition than Henry IV had.

Henry V has in him something of his father, and something of Hotspur. Has he not also in him, as king, something beneficial that he has retained from the old Eastcheap way of life? It was a wrong way of life, certainly: but did it not perhaps, in spite of its evil, help Henry V to develop that genuine fellow-feeling with the humblest of his subjects which impresses us so much at Agincourt? Did it not have in it, submerged under the evil which had to be cast off, that valuable element which he retained?

> Forth he goes and visits all his host,
> Bids them good morrow with a modest smile
> And calls them brothers, friends and countrymen . . . .
> Every wretch, pining and pale before,
> Beholding him, plucks comfort from his looks:
> A largess universal like the sun

K

His liberal eye doth give to every one,
Thawing cold fear, that mean and gentle all
Behold, as may unworthiness define,
A little touch of Harry in the night.
                    (*Henry V*, IV, prol. 32–4, 41–7)

Could Henry IV have done this? Could Hotspur?—Hotspur
would have been magnificent, but he would have tended to
rant rather, to talk resplendently—he would not have worn a
"modest smile". Of a surety no one like Falstaff could possibly
have behaved so! But does Henry V not owe *something* of
that fellow-feeling with the humble to the old way of life
which as a whole he so rightly sloughed off?

·   ·   ·   ·   ·

The essentials of the design of the trilogy may perhaps
(at the risk of repetition on the one hand and over-simplifi-
cation on the other) be stated as follows. We begin with a
thoroughly bad king—a disordered personality in which "will
doth mutiny with wit's regard." He produces disorder in the
state by unkingly conduct. England is being ruined by him.
To continue to tolerate him is to invite further ruin. But to
depose him would be a crime against the law of God. England
is in a dilemma. The true moral course is for her to endure
Richard, to leave him to God's vengeance for betrayal of
trust, even if she has to accept the role of martyrdom.

But he *is* deposed—that crime is committed: and then
he is murdered. Henry IV becomes king. Though coming
to the throne by a disorderly deed, he wants to produce order
in the kingdom. In his personality will does not mutiny with
wit's regard; but he is a guilty man, and he is dogged by
Nemesis. He has to contend with rebellion from his former
supporters: prophecies of woe uttered by Richard and others
are fulfilled: and the dissoluteness of his son and heir may be
thought of as part of the retribution for the crime of usurpation.
It looks as if when Henry V becomes king he will be like
Richard, and as if he will be deposed in his turn by Hotspur
or another such. But the Prince, a prodigal son figure, repents
and emerges as the good king *par excellence*. He embraces

the ideal of law and order which he had previously flouted. But more than this. The *Richard II* and *Henry IV* plays present us with various kinds of character and various ways of life, and we find ourselves comparing them in the light of the question, what is the nature of the ideal king?

Richard, though legitimately king, is disfigured by personality disorder. Henry IV has no such personality disorder as Richard. He uses "policy", and we feel that calculation, keeping his eye on the main chance, is too prominent a part of his character for us to sympathize with him fully. He is not sufficiently warm-hearted. Hotspur detests him as a "vile politician". But Hotspur is open to criticism on other grounds. If Hotspur were ever to become king he would not be successful. He is animated by a noble ideal of chivalric honour, but he is immoderate, rash, imprudent, lacking in discretion. Hotspur is criticized by, among others, Falstaff (who is opposed to Henry IV's values also). Falstaff, the misleader of youth, represents a way of life that culminates in diseases. The prince rightly gives it up. But from it, it may be suggested, he retains a sense of fellow-feeling with the humble and low which contributes beneficially to his character as king. We have a chain of character-comparisons: as regards values, we have Henry IV opposed to Richard II; opposed to Henry IV we have, in different ways, Hotspur and Falstaff; Falstaff is opposed to Hotspur; and Falstaff himself is rejected. The ideal king, Henry V, exemplifies both "policy" and chivalry, but he is not a second Henry IV nor a second Hotspur. Something of both there is in him: but, unlike either of them, he is a properly balanced personality, a sympathetically conceived order-figure. If at one point he talks as Henry IV might, he is yet, unlike Henry IV, essentially a frank and warm-hearted personality, a fully human personality. If at another point he talks as Hotspur might, he is yet, unlike Hotspur, a man of judgment and discretion.

.   .   .   .   .

We have said that Henry V is Shakespeare's conception of the ideal king. It must be admitted that not all critics find themselves able to give him unqualified admiration. Their reasons, however, do not seem to me valid.

In Act I, scene ii, of *Henry V*, Henry asks the Archbishop of Canterbury to declare whether or not his, Henry's, claim against France is justifiable. "May I with right and conscience make this claim?" he asks. He is fully aware of the terrible consequences of war, and he charges the Archbishop "in the name of God" to speak the truth, to speak "justly and religiously". "For," he says,

> we will hear, note and believe in heart
> That what you speak is in your conscience wash'd
> As pure as sin with baptism.
>
> (*Henry V*, I, ii, 30-2)

We note the religious tone. Later in the scene Henry claims to be a "Christian king". But some critics would accuse him of hypocrisy in this scene. If they are right, we cannot accord him unqualified admiration.

In Act I, scene i, we learn that a project which had, in Henry IV's reign, been advanced and dropped has now been advanced again—a project for the confiscation of temporal lands which have passed into the Church's possession by bequest. This project is being urged by the Commons. The king "seems indifferent"—if anything rather more favourable towards the Church than towards those urging the bill. For, the Archbishop says, he—the Archbishop—has offered the king a large sum of money from the Church's coffers to help in the waging of a war against France. He has done so, of course, to predispose the king against the bill or to distract his attention from it. He has apparently indicated to the king that such a war is justifiable:

> I have made an offer to his majesty,
> Upon our spiritual convocation
> And in regard of causes now in hand,
> Which I have open'd to his grace at large,
> As touching France, to give a greater sum
> Than ever at one time the clergy yet
> Did to his predecessors part withal.
>
> (*Henry V*, I, i, 75-81)

And so, some critics say, when in I, ii, Henry asks the
Archbishop to declare whether he has just claims on France,
he knows that the Archbishop, for self-interest, *wants* him
to go to war, and so he knows that the Archbishop will say
the claims are just whether they are or not. And thus Henry
is laid open to the charge of being a hypocrite. Bradley says
that "when [Henry] adjures the Archbishop to satisfy him as
to his right to the French throne, he knows very well that
the Archbishop *wants* the war, because it will defer and perhaps
prevent what he considers the spoliation of the Church."
And, before Bradley, Swinburne had said: "The supple and
shameless egotism of the churchmen on whose political
sophistries [Henry] relies for external support is needed
rather to varnish his project than to reassure his conscience."[1]
We are not here concerned with actual history: we are not
concerned with Holinshed's Chronicle, Shakespeare's source:
we are concerned solely with Shakespeare's play. Is Henry
indicated by Shakespeare as a hypocrite?

I believe that the most that can be said is that Shakespeare
presents the matter in such a way that a given reader might,
if he wished, choose to regard Henry as hypocritical here.
Let us consider the facts as they appear from the text of the
play. The Archbishop, as we learn from I, i, offered Henry
the money in an interview which was interrupted by the
arrival of an embassy from France. This embassy is received
by Henry in I, ii. The ambassadors bring back a reply from
the Dauphin to a claim Henry has made to certain French
dukedoms. Apparently he has not yet claimed the French
throne. Before the interview at which the Archbishop offered
the money, then, Henry had already claimed the dukedoms.
Now in I, ii, before the admittance of the ambassadors, Henry
questions the Archbishop, in front of the court, as to the validity
of his claim to—what? Clearly to the French *throne*. It is
obvious that by I, ii, 263 and 275, Henry has formed the
intention of securing the French crown. Now, if his original
claim was restricted to certain dukedoms, when did he first
definitely conceive the idea of claiming the French throne?

---

[1] Both passages are quoted on p. xix of the introduction to Professor
Dover Wilson's edition of *Henry V*, where this matter is discussed.

At the interview between Henry and the Archbishop, referred to in I, i, the Archbishop had "opened" certain "causes" regarding France to the king. Henry at that interview showed a willingness to hear

> The severals and unhidden passages
> Of his true titles to some certain dukedoms
> And generally to the crown and seat of France.
> (*Henry V*, I, i, 86–8)

The suggestion is, apparently, that, whereas Henry had already claimed the dukedoms, the Archbishop incited him to go on and claim the crown as well, and offered him financial help for reasons that Henry must have realized clearly enough. It could be argued, then, that in I, ii, Henry's request for the Archbishop's opinion is, in fact, disingenuous. Swinburne and Bradley take it so.

They are counsel for the prosecution. I believe that counsel for the defence could put up a winning case. The fact is that whereas Swinburne's and Bradley's interpretation admittedly fits in with the text, the contrary opinion—that Henry was being perfectly sincere—is equally tenable. We might equally well take it that Henry originally claimed the dukedoms in perfectly good faith—then the Archbishop suggested to him that he claim the crown as well—he knew that the Archbishop had special motives for doing so—and therefore in I, ii, he made a special point of conjuring the Archbishop very solemnly to speak the truth as to the validity of the English claim to the French throne. I believe that I, i and ii, *could* be interpreted in this way. And so we have this position: either interpretation could stand, if we took I, i and ii, by themselves: now, if we take the play as a whole, Henry is unquestionably presented sympathetically in general: it is reasonable therefore in I, ii, to give him the benefit of the doubt and regard him as speaking perfectly sincerely.

.   .   .   .

Another ground upon which some readers might feel inclined to criticize Henry adversely is his treatment of his prisoners at Agincourt. At IV, vi, 34, an alarum sounds. Henry

ealizes that "the French have reinforced their scatter'd
nen", and he goes on:

> Then every soldier kill his prisoners:
> Give the word through.

Some might say that this was indeed a reprehensibly harsh
order from a most "Christian king". But surely Shakespeare's
audiences would not have thought so. The English army was
outnumbered by the French: a French rally was very
dangerous: such a difficult position demanded drastic pre-
cautions by the English commander-in-chief. Shakespeare
without doubt intended Henry's ruthlessness here to be
regarded as commendable. This point is well put by Professor
Dover Wilson in his edition of the play.

．　　．　　．　　．　　． ．

Before we leave *Henry V* there is one more point which
must be dealt with. In this play we have an actor, called the
Chorus, who gives a speech before each act, and an epilogue
at the end. The speeches of the Chorus, the Prologues to the
various acts, indicate that in this play Shakespeare is profoundly concerned with the idea that the resources of his
stage are inadequate for the realization of the purposes he
has in view. Dissatisfaction with his medium is clearly
indicated in such passages as these:

> Can this cockpit hold
> The vasty fields of France? or may we cram
> Within this wooden O the very casques
> That did affright the air at Agincourt?
> > (I Prologue, 11–14)

> And so our scene must to the battle fly;
> Where—O for pity!—we shall much disgrace
> With four or five most vile and ragged foils,
> Right ill-disposed in brawl ridiculous,
> The name of Agincourt.
> > (IV Prologue, 48–52)

The Chorus keeps appealing to the audience to use its
imagination. The resources of the stage do not permit of the
presentation of anything approaching the real thing.

In addition, the Chorus indicates changes of place to the audience—it explicitly announces a shift from England to France or vice versa. It describes episodes and movements which take place during the story but are not enacted on the stage: and some of the description is of movements that could not be represented on any stage—for instance, the sailing of the English fleet for France, described in the Prologue to Act III.

Now in no other play does Shakespeare seem perturbed by the thought that the resources of his stage are inadequate. Why in this play in particular? He has other plays involving armies and battles—he has other plays involving movement over wide areas. Why is he discontented with his medium in this particular case and not, apparently, in others?

The answer to this question is furnished by Mr. A. H. Tolman in an essay included in his book *Falstaff and Other Shakespearean Topics* (1925). In connection with this answer let us bear in mind two things—(i) Henry V is Shakespeare's ideal king, and Shakespeare's ideal king is a warrior-king, a hero-king, and (ii) Henry is a perfectly balanced personality: he has his spiritual troubles, certainly: things do not always go completely smoothly for him: his mind is sometimes clouded by disappointment or by anger or by the weight of his responsibilities: but there is no psychological war within him: there is no civil strife in the kingdom of his personality.

Now to give a full and true impression of a great warrior-king the dramatist has to show him in actual warlike action; and if the audience is to get the impression of a really splendid hero it is important that it should not feel that the action it sees on the stage is feeble or tawdry. Yet on the stage one cannot give any really adequate representation of, say, a great battle. Hence Shakespeare's anxiety. In no other play of his is the external action of such vital importance *in itself*.

Take, by way of contrast, *Antony and Cleopatra*. Here we have the scene shifting over a wider area than in *Henry V*. Here we have warlike action, too. But in *Antony and Cleopatra* Shakespeare's primary interest is in the conflicting impulses and emotions in the hearts of the principal characters. This is highly dramatic material, and external action has not vital importance *in itself*. In *Henry V* things are different. The presentation of the hero-king, who has no large-scale spiritual agonies and no psychological irregularities, necessitates the presentation of action in a splendid way: the external action has importance in itself: and of course the stage is inadequate. To this extent the material of *Henry V* is, as Mr. Tolman holds, not so much dramatic as epic. Shakespeare is in this case trying to present in dramatic form material which is, at any rate in some places, epic rather than dramatic. And this is why he is troubled.

It may, perhaps, be said that he has pushed himself into a corner. When he embarked on *Richard II* he was embarking on a *set* of plays. The material of *Richard II* and *I and II Henry IV* is intensely dramatic—the *main* interest is not in external action but rather in what occurs within the minds and hearts of the principal characters. But the culmination of the series of plays is the emergence of an ideal character of a type for the proper exhibition of which epic would offer advantages over drama.

In the Prologue to Act III of *Henry V* we have a picture of the magnificence of the English fleet as it sets sail for France. The passage reads like a piece of straightforward narrative-descriptive poetry, non-dramatic. We are even shown the ship-boys climbing on the rigging—we are given details like that. Shakespeare wants us to have a vivid detailed impression of the spectacle in order that we may appreciate properly the kind of action that characterizes a figure like Henry V. He sets the description outside the drama—it is simply recited by the Chorus.

Now we may remember Enobarbus's description of Cleopatra in her barge. That picture too has to be described—such a spectacle cannot be successfully presented on the stage. But Enobarbus's description occurs within stage-dialogue. In *Henry V*, I suppose, Shakespeare *could* have had one character describing to another the departure of the English fleet. He actually puts the description outside the drama proper. Surely the difference is that in *Antony and Cleopatra* he is dealing primarily with dramatic material, and where he has to give a piece of pure description he can simply put it in the mouth of one of the characters: whereas in *Henry V* the description has a cardinal importance in itself which makes Shakespeare feel that the best thing to do is simply to write a piece of straightforward narrative-descriptive poetry and set it outside the drama, thus virtually *admitting* that his material is in a very real sense non-dramatic.

There is extant a play called *The Famous History of the Life and Death of Captain Thomas Stukeley*, written probably before *Henry V* was. In this play of Stukeley we have a Chorus which performs the same functions as that in *Henry V*. Thus, at one point the Chorus in *Stukeley* says:

> Thus of Alcazar's battle in one day
> Three kings at once did lose their hapless lives.
> Your gentle favour must we needs entreat
> For rude presenting such a royal fight,
> Which more imagination must supply
> Than all our utmost strength can reach unto.
> Suppose the soldiers who you saw surprised
> The poor dismayed prince Antonio
> Have sold him to the wealthy Moor they talk'd of,
> And that such time as needs must be allowed
> Already he hath passed in servitude.
> Sit now and see unto our story's end
> All those mishaps that this poor prince attend.
>
>   (R. Simpson, *The School of Shakspere*, 1878, Vol. I, p. 264)[1]

Here we have the Chorus apologizing for the "rude presenting" of a great battle—referring to the need for the audience to use its imagination—telling the audience of events in the story that intervene between episodes actually presented on the stage. The Chorus in *Henry V* does all this, too. But if Shakespeare copied the artifice from the Stukeley play, I think it was not a case simply of copying without a specific reason: it may well be that Shakespeare, realizing that in *Henry V* he had to deal with the problem that we have discussed, remembered this play of *Stukeley* and its Chorus, and realized that here was his solution.

Mr. Tolman is right in calling our attention to "the epic character of *Henry V*". And the fact that *Henry V* partakes

---

[1] I have supplied some punctuation.

of this character is the reason why it makes such admirable material for film treatment. The particular stage limitations that Shakespeare deplores are conspicuously absent from the art of the cinema. The cinema *can* present the battle of Agincourt in a way that closely resembles the real thing. It is the real thing that Shakespeare wants:

> can this cockpit hold
> The vasty fields of France? or may we cram
> Within this wooden O the very casques
> That did affright the air at Agincourt?

No. But the cinema can give us something very close to the vasty fields of France, something very like the very casques themselves. I am sure that the ghost of Shakespeare applauded Sir Laurence Olivier's resolve to film *Henry V*. And the film was, on the whole, a resplendent success.[1] But *Henry V* is a special case—and the reaction of the ghost of Shakespeare to the idea of filming *Hamlet* may perhaps have been rather different.

.   .   .   .   .

I have tried to show that this great sequence of plays embodies a coherent design or pattern, as Dr. Johnson long ago saw it did. At the beginning, as we have seen, we have, among other things, a rebellion against a bad king: and that rebellion is presented by Shakespeare, unequivocally, as a sin. It should be pointed out, however, that there were, in Shakespeare's day, two schools of thought regarding the defensibility of rebellion against a bad king. And Shakespeare, in his plays, makes use now of the one, now of the other. One school of thought held that rebellion was a sin in all cases, even against a bad ruler. This is reflected by Shakespeare in this trilogy. The other held that a wicked and unjust ruler might legitimately be attacked: and this is reflected in Shakespeare when, for instance, the evil king Richard III encounters rebellion, or when Cordelia and the French forces proceed

[1] Though I do not think that the Archbishop of Canterbury should have been presented as a comic character in I, ii.

against Goneril, Regan, and their supporters.[1] With this footnote we must leave Shakespeare and History and consider Shakespeare and Tragedy, though these are not, of course, mutually exclusive terms, since Shakespeare conceives of the play of *Richard II* as a tragedy.

[1] On this matter see John F. Danby, *Shakespeare's Doctrine of Nature* (1949), p. 78.

CHAPTER VI

TRAGEDY

SHAKESPEARIAN Tragedy is such a tremendous subject that it is difficult to see how to handle it within the restricted limits of a book of this size. The same great order-disorder antithesis with which we have dealt in Comedy and History lies at the heart of the tragedies; and in the present chapter I propose to confine myself for the most part to illustrating this by an analysis of two examples—*Macbeth* and *Coriolanus*. I take *Macbeth* first.

The disorder-atmosphere of the play is suggested at the outset in a brief but masterly opening scene. The initial stage direction indicates thunder and lightning: there is disorder in the physical universe. Three creatures, called Witches in the stage direction, enter. The first says:

> When shall we three meet again?
> In thunder, lightning, or in rain?

The two question marks appear in the first edition of the play (in the collected edition of Shakespeare's plays published in folio in 1623); but I agree with those commentators—the majority—who regard the first one as an error. As the punctuation stands, the speaker seems to be saying, "When shall we three meet again? Shall we meet in thunder, or shall we meet in lightning, or shall we meet in rain?" I cannot think this is Shakespeare's intention. Surely the compositor's eye has caught the question mark at the end of line 2 too soon: he has set it up at the end of line 1, and has then repeated it in its proper place. The first Witch, then, says:

> When shall we three meet again
> In thunder, lightning, or in rain?

The suggestion is that they always meet in conditions of tempest. When they meet, the universe is always in a condition of disorder—because they themselves are disorder-figures. It is the doctrine of correspondences again. They always meet in conditions of tempest, then: when are they to do so again?

The second Witch replies:

> When the hurlyburly's done,
> When the battle's lost and won.

And thus we learn of another disorder: a battle is going on—disorder on the plane of human society. The Witches will meet again when the battle is over. The word "hurlyburly" conveys the disorder-idea extremely effectively, with its suggestion of confusion and turmoil. We may note also another point in connection with this speech of the second Witch. I hope it will not seem to the reader too far-fetched. Her second line has a perfectly rational meaning: one side will win the battle, the other will lose it. But apart from this rational meaning the wording suggests something else to the mind of the sophisticated reader or hearer. At its end the battle will be both lost and won—it will be both one thing and its opposite. This suggests the disorder that consists in a confusion between opposites which is re-echoed more significantly a little later when the Witches say "Fair is foul, and foul is fair". In the line "When the battle's lost and won" Shakespeare uses a phrase with a perfectly commonplace significance, but he patterns the words in such a way as to give at the same time another significance, an imaginative significance which the sensitive reader or auditor will appreciate.

The Witches, then, will meet again when the battle is over. "That will be ere the set of sun," says the third Witch. And already we feel that we are in the presence of supernaturally endowed creatures gifted with prophecy. We are in the presence of creatures of disorder who have connections with what we may call cosmic forces of disorder. The atmosphere of the supernatural is reinforced by the ritualistic question-and-answer form that the dialogue takes:

> 1st Witch. Where the place?
> 2nd Witch.   Upon the heath.
> 3rd Witch. There to meet with Macbeth.

It is important to notice that these supernaturally endowed creatures of disorder are going to take the initiative—they are going to waylay the hero, obviously for evil purposes as the thunder and lightning themselves are sufficient to indicate. Supernatural evil is going deliberately to bring itself to bear on a human being.

Then the Witches respond to the calls of their familiar spirits: [1]

> *1st Witch.* I come, Graymalkin!
> *2nd Witch.* Paddock calls.
> *3rd Witch.* Anon.

Graymalkin is a cat, Paddock a toad: the reference is to two evil spirits which take the forms of animals in order to establish contact with the Witches who are themselves actually human.

Finally the Witches all chorus:

> Fair is foul, and foul is fair:
> Hover through the fog and filthy air.

The weather conditions are again indicated, reinforcing the impression of disorder. And the appalling principle of reversal voiced by the Witches—"Fair is foul, and foul is fair"—clearly indicates what they represent. They represent the sort of disorder that consists of inversion. What is good according to the law of nature and order is to them evil: what is evil according to that law is to them good. They are like Milton's Satan, who cries out "Evil, be thou my good". These Witches believe that fair is foul and foul is fair: they are going to waylay the hero of the play: already we may well suspect that they are deliberately seeking out a good man ("fair") in order to turn him into an evil man ("foul").

Disorder in the physical elements—disorder amongst men (the battle)—the Witches, human disorder-figures who are controlled by supernatural disorder-forces, about to seek out a good man to pervert him in accordance with their detestable principle of inversion: all this, within the economical limits of eleven short lines, creates the atmosphere, the *milieu*, of the play; and the dramatic art that has gone into the making of the scene is masterly.

[1] The distribution of the speeches here is editorial. The original folio has errors.

In the second scene a picture is painted for us of Macbeth as the valiant upholder of order—the brave defender of his rightful king against invasion and rebellion. The impression is powerfully conveyed to us of a hero who is a great order-figure.

The encounter between the Witches and Macbeth takes place in I, iii. Macbeth enters, with Banquo; and Macbeth's first words—"So foul and fair a day I have not seen"—carry our minds back to the opening scene. Just as in the case of the second Witch's words about the battle being lost and won, so here the words have a perfectly rational meaning: the day is foul in that the weather is bad, but it is fair in that a great victory has been won by the army in which Macbeth was a prominent officer. But again, apart from this rational meaning, the pattern of the words has imaginative significance. We remember the Witches' chorus of "Fair is foul, and foul is fair", and we are reminded of all that we learned in that scene. Macbeth, the order-figure, is about to be ambushed by disorder-figures intent on perverting him.

The encounter takes place, then. Macbeth asks the Witches to speak, if they can, and they greet him:

> *1st Witch.* All hail, Macbeth! hail to thee, thane of Glamis!
> *2nd Witch.* All hail, Macbeth! hail to thee, thane of Cawdor!
> *3rd. Witch* All hail, Macbeth, that shalt be king hereafter!
> (I, iii, 48–50)

What is Macbeth's reaction to this? We learn it from Banquo's mouth. Macbeth is rapt. Hearing the Witches' words he starts, and seems "to fear Things that do sound so fair" (I, iii, 51–52). That word "fair" echoes Macbeth's use of it a moment before— "So foul and fair a day I have not seen", which in turn recalls I, i. And so we may legitimately think in the following terms: the Witches' prophecies sound fair, but, by the inversion of which we have spoken, we, audience and readers, can realize already that they are actually to be associated with foulness, with evil. We immediately realize that if Macbeth becomes king it will involve disorder, not a legitimate elevation to the throne.

But we must consider Macbeth's own reaction to the Witches' greeting. As we have said, he is afraid. He is also fascinated—when they vanish he wishes they had stayed. Now the keynote of fear recurs again and again. In the latter half of I, iii, Ross and Angus enter to tell Macbeth that he has been created thane of Cawdor. The lesser of the Witches' prophecies having been fulfilled so promptly, as if by Fate, Macbeth naturally cannot help thinking of the possibility of the greater also being fulfilled. And again, at that thought, he is afraid. At I, iii, 130 ff., he speaks of his hair standing on end and his heart knocking against his ribs contrary to nature. Why do these things happen to him? Because already he is thinking in terms of becoming king by murdering Duncan, the rightful sovereign. Can we not conjecture that his initial fear, registered as soon as the Witches have spoken, was caused by his realizing even then, even so soon, the nature of the deed in which the fulfilment of the final prophecy would involve him? In I, iv, Duncan names his son Malcolm as his successor: and Macbeth definitely, at least for the time being, resolves on the murder:

> Stars, hide your fires;
> Let not light see my black and deep desires:
> The eye wink at the hand; yet let that be,
> Which the eye fears, when it is done, to see.
>
> (I, iv, 50-3)

But again we note the word "fear". And when he has actually committed the murder we have him saying:

> I am afraid to think what I have done.
>
> (II, ii, 51)

It seems clear, then, that on hearing the Witches' salutations Macbeth's mind is the scene of a severe conflict. On the one hand he would like to be king, even though he realizes from the start what evil that may involve: on the other hand he is mortally afraid of the deed—he is terrified even by the thought of it.

Now in I, vii, he delivers a soliloquy which is a crucial piece of self-revelation. And it is near enough to the beginning of the play to allow us to carry our minds right back and realize fully the explanation of Macbeth's reaction to the Witches' salutations and to the succeeding events (his becoming thane of Cawdor, and Duncan's naming of Malcolm as heir).

L

In the soliloquy in question, Macbeth finishes up by con-
fessing that he is animated by an overweening ambition:

> I have no spur
> To prick the sides of my intent, but only
> Vaulting ambition, which o'erleaps itself
> And falls on the other—
>
> (I, vii, 25-8)

And falls, presumably, on the other side of the horse on to
which it is attempting to jump. Macbeth, then, is improperly
ambitious: and he knows it. That is our first point.

We observe that in the lines just quoted Macbeth foresees
failure. His ambition is of a kind which does not get into the
saddle, which does not succeed. Now earlier in the soliloquy
he has been speaking of the probability of his not being able
to commit the murder without being detected and brought to
judgment by his fellow-countrymen. What Macbeth is saying
in this soliloquy is this—this is his main thought—"If I could
commit this murder and succeed in escaping detection by my
fellow-men, I would not worry about a possible condemnation
for it in the life to come. But what worries me is that I may
be found out *in this world:* I may be arraigned and condemned
for murder." These are the ideas which preoccupy him, on
the conscious level; and it is to be noted that when, at the end
of the scene, Lady Macbeth tells him that she has devised a
plan of action which will make detection at any rate most
unlikely, Macbeth resolves finally on the deed. It is clear that
the possibility of retribution on this side of the grave is all
that he *thinks* is troubling him. And in the soliloquy he professes himself to be a disorder-figure: he professes himself to
be one who would "jump the life to come".

But, though he knows that his ambition is overweening,
he is nevertheless lacking in self-knowledge. For the *imagery*
of the soliloquy shows that what is *really* troubling him, deep
down, is not what he *thinks* is troubling him. He speaks of
"angels, trumpet-tongued" pleading against "the deep
damnation" of Duncan's "taking-off". And he speaks of Pity,

> like a naked new-born babe,
> Striding the blast, or heaven's cherubim, horsed
> Upon the sightless couriers of the air,

blowing "the horrid deed in every eye". The imagery is
religious—apocalyptic. It brings to our minds the idea of the
awfulness of the Last Judgment. While Macbeth is saying, is
consciously thinking, that he is troubled only by the idea of
earthly retribution, that he would "jump the life to come",
his imagination is actually filled with images which suggest
the Day of Judgment. In other words, deep down within
himself, he *is* very much preoccupied with the life to come.
I think we may legitimately use the terminology of modern
psychology and say that in his subconscious mind Macbeth is
terrified by the notion of himself condemned by God. For,
fundamentally, he *believes in* the law of God, the law of
nature, the law of order. And he is terrified by the idea of
upsetting it. And so we look back and realize that the picture
of Macbeth presented in I, ii, was essentially a true picture: he
is esssentially an order-figure at the outset. And we realize
the reason for his fear whenever, from the very start, he thinks
of the possibility or necessity of committing murder.

He does commit the murder, of course. And in his description of that to his wife, in II, ii, we have a further illustration
of his fundamental belief in order, of his fundamental desire
to stand well with God. He describes how, on his way to do
the deed, he passed a room in which one cried "God bless
us!" and another "Amen!". "Listening their fear," he says,

> I could not say 'Amen',
> When they did say 'God bless us!'

And he goes on:

> But wherefore could not I pronounce 'Amen'?
> I had most need of blessing, and 'Amen'
> Stuck in my throat.

(II, ii, 29–33)

Now at first hearing we might be tempted to say, what a fool
this Macbeth is! He wonders why, on his way to murder his
king, his kinsman, his guest, he is unable to say "Amen" to
the exclamation "God bless us". He even appears to think
himself entitled to God's blessing when engaged on such an
errand! He is puzzled by his inability to pronounce that

"Amen". Yet he knows well enough that what he is bent on is the commission of a heinous crime. I should be perfectly prepared to admit that Shakespeare means us to understand that Macbeth is a fool. Macbeth wants to eat his cake and have it. He wants to kill his king and be blessed by God in the very moment of doing so.

A fool, certainly. But the reason I cite the passage here is that it shows that even as he goes to do the criminal deed Macbeth, in his heart, believes in the law of order that he is destroying. The deed is contrary to his own deepest convictions. These convictions are so strong an element in him that they assert themselves even at such a moment and even though they impel him to absurdity. It is a vivid testimony to their strength. As he damns himself he wants blessing, despite all that reason could have told him. And then, after the murder has been committed, he says: "I am afraid to think what I have done" (II, ii, 51). Fear again.

I have been stressing the view of Macbeth as essentially an order-figure who acts contrary to his own innermost convictions. Remembering the opening scene of the play, where the Witches indicated their intention of taking the initiative and ambushing the hero, are we to say that Macbeth is simply pushed on to evil by external forces—the Witches' prophecies, the fatal fact that the lesser prophecy is at once fulfilled, and the persuasions of his strong-minded wife? Is he simply a noble hero, a perfectly innocent man, who is victimized, perverted, by outside forces? I should not say quite that.

I believe that we must be careful to keep properly balanced two distinct factors. In an earlier chapter, in another connection, we discussed the play of *Othello*. We saw that in that play the hero is a victim of an outside force—Iago. Had Iago not pushed Othello on, there would have been no tragedy. On the other hand, we also saw that, even before the jealousy motif ever arose, there was evidence that Othello, a noble figure, had in his personality a *potentiality* to evil: we saw that in a moment of crisis he himself confessed that his passions were striving to overthrow his reason. Had he not been a person in whom this was liable to happen, Iago could have had no success in his manipulation of him.

The tragedy in *Othello* is caused by two forces working in conjunction: it is caused by an external force of evil deliberately bringing itself to bear on a noble figure which has within it a *seed* of evil. The external evil force fertilizes that seed of evil. It is essentially the same with Macbeth, I am sure. I have claimed that at the outset Macbeth is essentially an order-figure. But I take it that deep down within him there is a seed of evil. The influence of external forces of evil is brought to bear on him, and that influence fertilizes the seed, which would not have germinated without it.

If we say that the Witches, taking the initiative, are intent on tempting Macbeth, we may say also that Macbeth reacts positively to the temptation with remarkable speed. If he were, so to speak, an order-figure without complications he would reject the Witches and their prophecies altogether and at once. He would perhaps laugh them off, or dismiss them with indignation. But, despite his fundamental belief in order, he does not do so. True, at I, iii, 143-4, he may say:

> If chance will have me king, why, chance may crown me,
> Without my stir.

But he does not really believe it. We notice the tentative word "may": and only a few lines later he is saying to Banquo:

> Think upon what hath chanced, and, at more time,
> The interim having weigh'd it, let us speak
> Our free hearts each to other.
>
> (I, iii, 153-5)

He has just said that chance may crown him; but here, a moment or two later, he is looking forward to a conference with Banquo, surely because he really knows that he will have to do something himself, and is anxious not to have to undertake an evil and dangerous act alone.

As I see it, right from the very moment when the Witches accost him, Macbeth is in the grip of a mental conflict. On the one hand, his fundamental belief in order causes him to react with fear to suggestions that he understands perfectly clearly from the start. On the other hand, that seed of evil of which we have spoken *is* stirred into life by the Witches' words. A conflict ensues between his impulse to maintain order and his impulse to destroy it: and a bitter conflict it is. To the external influence of the Witches and the fate that fulfils their lesser prophecy is added the external influence of his wife. At times he resists the impulsion to destroy order: but actually this evil element prevails, and, though not without anguish and remorse, the deed is committed.

. . . . .

Before proceeding we must deal with one objection which some readers might make to what we have been saying. After the delivery of the soliloquy in I, vii, with which we have dealt, Lady Macbeth enters. Macbeth says: "We will proceed no further in this business". She taunts him with cowardice. He says that he dares "do all that may become a man". And she replies:

> What beast was't, then,
> That made you break this enterprise to me?
> When you durst do it, then you were a man;
> And, to be more than what you were, you would
> Be so much more the man. Nor time nor place
> Did then adhere, and yet you would make both:
> They have made themselves, and that their fitness now
> Does unmake you.
>
> (I, vii, 47–54)

She refers to a previous interview between them in which Macbeth had suggested to her that he, or they, should commit this murder. This interview took place at a time when Duncan was not in the castle, and, moreover, at a time when it was not known to the two of them that he would visit the castle. When could such an interview have taken place? If we look carefully through the play up to I, vii, we find that there is no place where such an interview could be supposed to take place. Must we then suppose that it took place before the beginning of the play? If so, Macbeth has deliberately proposed the murder before the Witches accosted him. That means that the Macbeth who so valiantly defends Duncan in the battle described in I, ii, is a hypocrite. He certainly cannot be described as essentially an order-figure. Are we then quite wrong in our analysis?

Is Shakespeare in I, ii, concerned with the appearance-

versus-reality theme? Is the picture of the hero painted in
that scene ironical? Is the idea of murdering his king already
in his heart? I cannot think so. I agree with the explanation
of I, vii, 47–54, given by Professor Dover Wilson in his edition
of the play. If Macbeth had already thought seriously and
deliberately of the murder, could he react to the idea of committing it as he does at I, iii, 130 ff. ? There he speaks of his
hair standing on end and of his heart knocking against his
ribs. Is this not obviously the reaction of a man who is brought face
to face with the idea of committing murder for the first time—an
idea, moreover, which is profoundly repugnant to him? I think so.

Professor Dover Wilson argues, to me convincingly, that
the play which we possess is not the *Macbeth* that Shakespeare
originally wrote. It is an abridgment. Some of the cutting—
not all—he believes to have been done by Shakespeare himself,
including the particular piece with which we are here concerned. He suggests that a scene has been cut out after I, iii,
a scene between Macbeth and his wife, in which Macbeth
tells her of what has happened and proposes the murder. The
idea is that Macbeth, who was on his way to Forres from Fife,
goes round by Inverness, interviews his lady, and then proceeds to Forres where he turns up in I, iv. If such a scene has
indeed been cut in the postulated abridgment, it follows that
the first part of I, v, has been interpolated as a substitution.

In the scene which, according to the theory, has been cut,
Macbeth presumably told Lady Macbeth about his encounter
with the Witches. In the play as we have it, she learns of the
encounter by means of the letter which she reads out at the
beginning of I, v. The latter then must be a substitution.
Presumably the substituted material is not of such length as
the cut scene was, the motive for the cutting being presumably
the shortening of the play. For a full discussion the reader is
referred to Dover Wilson's edition of the play. I think his
suggestion is a very good one, absolving us, as it does, from
the necessity of supposing that Macbeth had planned the
murder of Duncan before he ever met the Witches. I should
say it was quite probable that I, v, 1–31a could be regarded
as the substitution for the cut.

This theory of Dover Wilson's means that we must suppose

that immediately after I, iii, Macbeth goes to his wife and deliberately proposes the murder of Duncan. Could he do this so soon after reacting with extreme terror to the idea of committing the murder? I think so. Before the actual commission of the murder he oscillates between an inclination to commit it and an aversion to doing so. Thus at the end of I, iv, he has apparently resolved on the deed:

> yet let that be,
> Which the eye fears, when it is done, to see.
> (I, iv, 52–3)

But at the end of I, v, he says to his wife: "We will speak further", suggesting reluctance, a desire to put off the decision. At I, vii, 31, he tells his wife

> We will proceed no further in this business.

But at the end of the scene he can say

> I am settled, and bend up
> Each corporal agent to this terrible feat.

At I, iii, 130 ff., he is terrified by the thought of committing the deed. At the end of that same scene, however, he is saying to Banquo that they must consult together. I do not see that immediately after this, in the scene we suppose to have been cut, he cannot have been resolute for the murder, sufficiently so to be able to propose it to his wife. It is quite possible that after that his mind recoiled from the idea; thus when Duncan, in I, iv, named Malcolm as his successor, he had to make up his mind afresh to commit the murder:

> The Prince of Cumberland! that is a step
> On which I must fall down, or else o'erleap,
> For in my way it lies. Stars, hide your fires;
> Let not light see my black and deep desires:
> The eye wink at the hand; yet let that be,
> Which the eye fears, when it is done, to see.
> (I, iv, 48–53)

Professor Dover Wilson's theory of a cut scene fits in well with this motif of Macbeth oscillating between inclination to do the deed and aversion from doing it.

· · · · ·

Macbeth commits the murder, then, and becomes king.

And what he tries to do is to erect a structure of order on a foundation of disorder; and so does Lady Macbeth. Consider, for example, the banquet scene, III, iv, which takes place after Macbeth has committed not only the first but also a second murder—that of Banquo. Macbeth begins the scene by addressing his guests, who are his subjects:

> You know your own degrees; sit down: at first
> And last the hearty welcome.

Macbeth is a murderer, a disrupter of degree: but, having become king, he wants the kingdom to present the normal order-structure, in which the nobility naturally sits down at table in accordance with rank. The scene is symbolically significant, for the ghost of the murdered Banquo appears, to disturb Macbeth, and the banquet has to be broken up by Lady Macbeth saying to the guests:

> Stand not upon the order of your going,
> But go at once.
>
> (III, iv, 119–20)

The ghost of Banquo appears because of the evil that Macbeth has done: the appearance of the ghost makes the retention of the order-structure impossible. Bidden at the outset to sit down in order, the guests have at the end to be begged to leave pell-mell. And as regards the apparition itself, Macbeth protests against it because it is *unnatural*, contrary to the law of order.

> The time has been,
> That, when the brains were out, the man would die,
> And there an end; but now they rise again,
> With twenty mortal murders on their crowns,
> And push us from our stools: this is more strange
> Than such a murder is.
>
> (III, iv, 78–83)

("Strange" means "unnatural".) Having committed unnatural deeds in order to gain and retain the kingship, he wants the laws of nature to remain constant to their old ways in all other respects.

The same point can be illustrated by referring to the

comfort that Macbeth takes in the latter part of the play from
supernatural assurances that

> none of woman born
> Shall harm Macbeth,
>
> (IV, i, 80–1)

and that

> Macbeth shall never vanquish'd be until
> Great Birnam wood to high Dunsinane hill
> Shall come against him.
>
> (IV, i, 92–4)

The law of nature makes the idea of a man not born of woman
impossible to conceive (using the words in their normal sense,
as Macbeth understands them); the law of nature makes the
idea of a moving forest impossible to conceive (again using
the words in their normal sense, as Macbeth understands
them). So Macbeth takes refuge here in his confidence in the
law of nature—and he interprets the words in their natural,
their usual, senses. The law of nature is not of course violated
—it is in accordance with that law that an infant may be
untimely ripped from its mother's womb and survive; and of
course the forest does not really move. The significant point
is that Macbeth, as we have said, interprets the words in
their usual senses and that his faith in the law of order is
supreme.

We repeat—he wants to maintain the order-structure as it
was before, *except* that he is king and not subject. Shakespeare
shows that it cannot be done. Henry IV found that out; so
does Macbeth. I do not think that it would be wrong to say
that in the first half of the play we have a hero the coherence
and significance of whose life has been centred in his belief
in order. By the end of the play that significance has gone,
and he says:

> that which should accompany old age,
> As honour, love, obedience, troops of friends,
> I must not look to have.
>
> (V, iii, 24–6)

He cannot have the "order" which he wants—in which he
has always fundamentally believed. And a little later we have

his "To-morrow, and to-morrow, and to-morrow" speech
(V, v, 19 ff.), which shows that now he regards life as having
no significance, no meaning. He believed fundamentally in
order: the potentiality to evil which lay deep down within
him was awakened by external temptations and he committed
evil: he tried to build an order-structure on the basis of that
evil, on the basis of that disorder: he failed—inevitably—and
by the end of the play he has lost altogether the faith which
before had given his life significance.

.   .   .   .   .

We have seen that an important factor in this play is *conscience*. It is important not only in connection with Macbeth
but also in connection with Lady Macbeth. In a sense these
two characters change places in the play (and one wonders if
it would be too fanciful to relate this in an imaginative way to
the inversion theme which we have seen to be so important).

On receipt of Macbeth's letter in I, v, Lady Macbeth prays
to the spirits of darkness to remove from her all naturalness.
She deliberately seeks to become a disorder-figure. And up to
the time that the murder is committed she is the one who is
resolute for the deed, while Macbeth's conscience is troubling
him.

It is true that Lady Macbeth's unnaturalness is contrary
to the deepest characteristics of her being. She cannot kill
Duncan herself, because as he lies there asleep he reminds her
of her father: deep down in her heart nature does prevail. And
when in I, vii, she speaks these terrible words:

> I have given suck, and know
> How tender 'tis to love the babe that milks me:
> I would, while it was smiling in my face,
> Have pluck'd my nipple from his boneless gums,
> And dash'd the brains out, had I so sworn as you
> Have done to this—
>
> (lines 54–9)

the passage gives evidence again of the fact that in her heart,
deep down, nature holds sway: as Coleridge pointed out,[1] the

---
[1] Quoted by Dover Wilson in his edition, page 116.

passage, "though usually thought to prove a merciless and unwomanly nature, proves the direct opposite": for she is saying that rather than do what Macbeth has done she would do something in the last degree horrible—something that she regards as in the last degree horrible. She does know "how tender 'tis to love the babe that milks" her. The very fact that in I, v, itself she prays to be made unnatural might suggest that she knew that "compunctious visitings of nature" were liable to occur in her case.

Yet the fact remains that she is on the whole successful in suppressing the workings of nature in her heart as she urges her husband on to do the deed. Nature operates in both of them: but, while Macbeth has a severe back-and-forth struggle towards and against the deed, she is resolute for it. When it is done, and when, after the porter-scene, it is discovered, she collapses, faints, while Macbeth is able to assume a confident front. Critics admittedly disagree as to whether this faint of hers is genuine, or an artifice. For myself, I cannot think there is any doubt as to its genuineness. Sir Edmund Chambers is right, in my view, when he says that Macbeth here "acts consumately, touching just the right notes; the grief of the loving subject, the anger of the generous host. Banquo and Duncan's two sons alone see through the deception. On the other hand, Lady Macbeth's turn to give way comes in the very crisis of the action. Her fainting is not dissimulation; her nerves will bear no more."[1] Here the two of them have, as it were, changed places: he is firm—she gives way.

In Act III, scene ii, we have further indications of this exchange of roles—with Macbeth as the more positive of the two, Lady Macbeth as the more negative. She is not entirely negative, to be sure: she tells him to "be bright and jovial among your guests to-night"; but his reply shows *him* telling *her* what to do:

> So shall I, love; and so, I pray, be you:
> Let your remembrance apply to Banquo; etc.
>   (III, ii, 28–30)

And, a moment or two later, we have a consummate touch of

[1] The Warwick Shakespeare, *Macbeth*, p. 127.

Shakespearian art which effectively underlines what we are
trying to say. We have this piece of dialogue:

> *Macbeth.* Thou know'st that Banquo, and his Fleance, lives.
> *Lady Macbeth.* But in them nature's copy's not eterne.
> *Macbeth.* That's comfort yet; they are assailable;
> Then be thou jocund: ere the bat hath flown
> His cloister'd flight, ere to black Hecate's summons
> The shard-borne beetle with his drowsy hums
> Hath rung night's yawning peal, there shall be done
> A deed of dreadful note.
> *Lady Macbeth.*   What's to be done?
> *Macbeth.* Be innocent of the knowledge, dearest chuck,
> Till thou applaud the deed.
>   (III, ii, 37–46)

Let us note what happens here. Macbeth makes a statement,
to which Lady Macbeth replies with an innuendo (line 38).
Macbeth replies by giving her counsel as to her behaviour
and by telling her that a dreadful deed is to be done.
When she asks what it is, he will not tell her. This deed is to
be his affair.

Now this is almost exactly what we have earlier, in I, v,
but, as regards the speakers, the other way round. At I, v,
59 ff., we have this:

> *Macbeth.*   My dearest love,
> Duncan comes here to-night.
> *Lady Macbeth.*   And when goes hence?
> *Macbeth.* To-morrow, as he purposes.
> *Lady Macbeth.*   O, never
> Shall sun that morrow see!
> Your face, my thane, is as a book where men
> May read strange matters. To beguile the time,
> Look like the time; bear welcome in your eye,
> Your hand, your tongue: look like the innocent flower,
> But be the serpent under't. He that's coming
> Must be provided for: and you shall put
> This night's great business into my dispatch; . . .

Here it is Macbeth who makes use of an innuendo (line 61).
In her reply the Lady gives him counsel as to his
behaviour, and says that the deed to be done is her affair.

Comparing I, v, 59 ff., and III, ii, 37 ff., then, we have a remarkable piece of parallelism, with the active-passive roles reversed.

The former relationship is re-established temporarily at the banquet where the ghost of Banquo appears. Macbeth's behaviour here is caused by conscience, and Lady Macbeth speaks scornfully to him about it, and tries to strengthen him, as she did before when he was disinclined towards the murder of Duncan. But it is, as I say, just a temporary re-establishment of that relationship. At the end of the play, when Macbeth is rooted in evil, when he has lost his faith altogether in any positive value in life, we have Lady Macbeth collapsing entirely—we have the sleep-walking scene, and her death: in her, finally, the reverse has happened to what has happened in Macbeth's case: Macbeth has become completely hardened in wickedness, and the conscience that had been so active within him has died: Lady Macbeth, having had the initiative originally, has found conscience re-establishing itself within her. This alternation of the active-passive relationship is part of the pattern of the play.

· · · · ·

The play of *Macbeth*, then, finally, is based on the same order-disorder antithesis that we have studied in Comedy and History. We have a disordered hero in a disordered environment. And the order-disorder antithesis is treated in a story which calls forth in us far deeper emotions than any of the comedies do.

We have elsewhere spoken of *Othello*, and the reader is in a position to compare the tragic patterns of *Macbeth* and *Othello*. In *Othello* also we have a disordered hero and a disordered environment (the external disorder is represented by Iago). And the reader may also compare *King Lear*. Here at the start we are confronted with a hero who is clearly a disordered personality. He is defective in judgment. And this is not merely the effect of extreme age: "he hath ever but slenderly known himself": "the best and soundest of his time hath been but rash": and extreme age has aggravated the disorder. A disordered personality for a hero: and the hero in a disordered

environment. External to Lear, and affecting him, we have
the unnaturalness of Goneril and Regan. Parallel to the main
plot we have the sub-plot, concerning Gloucester (corresponding to Lear) and on the one hand Edgar (corresponding
to Cordelia) and on the other Edmund (corresponding to
Goneril and Regan). Had Lear not been lacking in judgment,
Goneril and Regan would never have had the power to do to
him what they did; had Goneril and Regan had natural feeling,
Lear's lack of judgment would not have issued in the tragedy
we have. Both factors are necessary. So also with Gloucester.
And so with Macbeth. Had he never met the Witches there
would have been no tragedy; but, equally, had the man
accosted by the Witches not had hidden within him a *seed*
of evil there would likewise have been no tragedy. So, at any
rate, the matter appears to me.

　　　　·　　　　　　·　　　　　　·

Let us now look in some detail at *Coriolanus*, a play
much less frequently read, I believe, than these others, and
a play treating, in its own way, the same fundamental
theme.

We are confronted at the very start with a hero who is
clearly a "humour character". He displays, very conspicuously,
a humour of pride, or self-love: he is an egotist. He is an
unbalanced, disordered character. He lacks temperateness; he
lacks soundness of judgment. Brutus and Sicinius, tribunes of
the plebs, are hostile to him: but his behaviour and speech are
frequently such as to make us feel that Brutus is substantially
right when, addressing Coriolanus, he says:

> 　　　　You speak o' the people,
> As if you were a god to punish, not
> A man of their infirmity.
> 　　　　(III, i, 80–2)

Brutus also—again correctly—characterizes him thus:

> 　　　　Being once chafed, he cannot
> Be rein'd again to temperance.
> 　　　　(III, iii, 27–8)

Again, Brutus sums him up excellently when he says:

> Caius Marcius was
> A worthy officer i' the war; but insolent,
> O'ercome with pride, ambitious past all thinking,
> Self-loving,—
>
> (IV, vi, 29-32)

This man Brutus, inimical to Coriolanus, admits that Coriolanus was "a worthy officer i' the war". He was. Coriolanus is brave: and there can be no doubt that he has in him elements of great nobility of character. This should be constantly borne in mind as we speak of him further and emphasize his weakness. He is a noble figure. But his pride is a cardinal fact of the play. And it ruins his whole personality. It brings down something potentially very great. We may well agree with Brutus's fellow-tribune, Sicinius, when he says of Coriolanus:

> I would he had continued to his country
> As he began, and not unknit himself
> The noble knot he made.
>
> (IV, ii, 30-2)

Coriolanus fights well, and Rome benefits. He appears to be fighting patriotically for Rome. Consider, for instance, how he inspires the Roman soldiery to follow his leadership:

> If any such be here—
> As it were sin to doubt—that love this painting
> Wherein you see me smear'd; if any fear
> Lesser his person than an ill report;
> If any think brave death outweighs bad life
> And that his country's dearer than himself;
> Let him alone, or so many so minded,
> Wave thus, to express his disposition,
> And follow Marcius.
>
> (I, vi, 67-75)

He speaks thus to the soldiers. But let us concentrate on one line of this passage. He exhorts to follow him anyone who thinks his country's dearer than himself. To think that would, of course, be to be truly patriotic. Does Coriolanus really think that his country's dearer than himself? The answer must be a negative one. Coriolanus, it must be said, thinks of his own honour more than he thinks of his country. And so we cannot

say that Coriolanus fights well for Rome, but must rather say
that Coriolanus fights well and Rome benefits, which is not
quite the same thing. At times he speaks like a patriot: "I have
done as you have done," he says to Titus Lartius, one of the
Roman generals:

> that's what I can; induced
> As you have been; that's for my country.
> (I, ix, 16–17)

But his own words elsewhere reveal him to us as not really a
patriot, but an egotist. Tullus Aufidius, general of the Volscians,
is an enemy of Rome; but he is also an enemy of Coriolanus,
not just because Coriolanus is a Roman—Aufidius is a private
enemy of Coriolanus. Coriolanus would like to defeat Aufidius.
Why? Not just because Coriolanus is a Roman and Aufidius a
Volscian. But also—and mainly—because Aufidius is Coriolanus's *own* enemy. To Coriolanus it is a matter of private
honour more than of patriotism. The claims of private honour
happen in this case to coincide with those of patriotism: but
(and this is vitally important) had it been that they clashed, it
would have been the claims of private honour that would have
won the day with the hero. His own words indicate this:

> Were half to half the world by the ears and he
> Upon my party, I'ld revolt, to make
> Only my wars with him.
> (I, i, 237–9)

I do not think that this is to be put down as rhetorical exag-
geration: Coriolanus really means it. His private honour means
more to him than his patriotism: and this is clearly seen again
after his banishment from Rome, when he declares that

> in mere spite,
> To be full quit of those my banishers,
> Stand I before thee [Aufidius] here.
> (IV, v, 88–90)

He has gone to his old enemy Aufidius, and offers him his
services against Rome:

> for I will fight
> Against my canker'd country with the spleen
> Of all the under fiends.
> (IV, v, 96–8)

M

This is essentially what Coriolanus has been all along—a man
who puts his private honour before his country's welfare.
Before his banishment he had declared that if Aufidius were
on his, Coriolanus's, side in the war then he, Coriolanus, would
revolt so as to be on the other side. His private honour demands
that he fight Aufidius and try to kill him. After his banishment his private honour demands that he fight against his
country in revenge. A nobler soul would still have held his
country's welfare high enough to prevent him actually leaguing
himself with her enemies, and, moreover, with his own former
personal enemy.

Aufidius is a renowned warrior; and it appears that the
basic reason for Coriolanus's special enmity towards him is
envy. In the first scene of the play Coriolanus says:

> I sin in envying his nobility,
> And were I any thing but what I am,
> I would wish me only he.
>
> (I, i, 234–6)

Aufidius is in a like case. To Coriolanus he says:

> Not Afric owns a serpent I abhor
> More than thy fame and envy.
>
> (I, viii, 3–4)

Each envies the other's personal fame as a warrior. It is vanity
which underlies this, of course. At the beginning of III, i,
Coriolanus asks Titus Lartius, "Saw you Aufidius?" Lartius
answers in the affirmative, and Coriolanus immediately asks,
"Spoke he of me?" "He did, my lord," says Lartius. "How?
what?" asks Coriolanus, with intense eagerness (III, i, 8–12).
Personal vanity could hardly be more clearly indicated.

Now, of course, patriotism is essentially consonant with
the order scheme. According to the order scheme, as we have
seen, *relation* was a vital concept. No created thing could be
regarded as isolated. Patriotism involves the concept of relation.
The individual is not an isolated entity—he stands in relation
to the whole state of which he is a member: he must remain
true to the position he has of right within it: he has privileges
and obligations: he has obligations to his fellow-citizens—the
warrior must fight for them all, not for himself only. Corio-

lanus is lacking in this essential morality of the order-figure. He is prepared to set order and nature aside in order to gratify his own ideals, in order to uphold his own honour.

It is surely his egotism, his humour of pride, that underlies that element in him which appears at first sight to be modesty. He does not like accepting rewards, indeed he does not like being thanked, even by persons whom he respects. After the Roman triumph over the Volsces in Act I there is to be a distribution of spoils among all the Roman soldiers involved. Cominius offers Coriolanus a special reward,

> to be ta'en forth,
> Before the common distribution.
>
> (I, ix, 34–5)

Coriolanus declines it:

> I thank you, general;
> But cannot make my heart consent to take
> A bribe to pay my sword: I do refuse it;
> And stand upon my common part with those
> That have beheld the doing.
>
> (I, ix, 36–40)

Those last dozen words are very revealing. This is not real modesty. It is a perverse pride. He will not consent to be thus distinguished from the other members of the army—but at the same time he is well aware of the difference between himself (who "did" indeed) and those who only "beheld the doing". He would certainly seem to be taking a perverse pleasure in equating himself as regards reward with others whom he regards as definitely inferior to himself. His perversity is seen again when he refuses even thanks for his exploits in the following words:

> I had rather have one scratch my head i' the sun
> When the alarum were struck than idly sit
> To hear my nothings monster'd.
>
> (II, ii, 79–81)

We cannot but detect a false note here. His military glory has been conspicuous. His deeds could by no stretch of licence be called "nothings". It is presumptuous in him to claim that they can. There is spiritual pride here. When someone thanks you for something you are in a sense under an obligation to him—you are indebted to him for his thanks which, after all, he *need* not give. But so great is Coriolanus's pride that he cannot bear to be under even that obligation. He is, in fact, in a pathological condition.

It is his sin of pride which is responsible for his banishment from Rome, for he has antagonized the commons by his passionate invective against them and their official representatives, the tribunes—invective full of unbearable insult, full of scurrility. He indeed speaks of and to the people as if he were a god to punish, not a man of their infirmity. Owing to his sin of pride he is banished: and as a result of the same proud egotism he resolves to join with Rome's enemies against her in revenge. That is to say, he shows himself to be one of those disorder-figures who place the satisfaction of their own individual desires above the law of order, the law of nature. The son of Rome takes up arms against her to satisfy his own pride, an unnatural proceeding. Emissaries from the city, pleading with him to spare it, are rejected by him. He rejects the demands made on him by his natural relationship to others. He makes himself stand isolated. In the end his mother, his wife, and his young son, with others, come to plead for Rome. As he sees them approaching, Coriolanus in soliloquy brutally states his resolve to be unnatural, to refuse the claims of his relationship to others:

> But out, affection!
> All bond and privilege of nature, break!
> Let it be virtuous to be obstinate.
>
> (V, iii, 24–6)

He rejects nature, and he shows up his own disorderliness by expressing an ethical inversion-principle (line 26). It is another case analogous to Satan's "Evil, be thou my good", or the Witches' "Fair is foul, and foul is fair" in *Macbeth*. "Let the Volsces," he says,

> Let the Volsces
> Plough Rome, and harrow Italy: I'll never
> Be such a gosling to obey instinct, but stand,
> As if a man were author of himself
> And knew no other kin.
>
> (V. iii, 33–7)

He resolves that he will behave as if he were indeed a phoenix
(to use John Donne's word). He resolves that he will
behave as if no other created thing had any claims on him.
But he cannot do it. He has himself stated a desire for inversion
("Let it be virtuous to be obstinate"); but the sight of an
inversion—mother kneeling to son—affects him profoundly:

> What is this?
> Your knees to me? to your corrected son?
> Then let the pebbles on the hungry beach
> Fillip the stars; then let the mutinous winds
> Strike the proud cedars 'gainst the fiery sun;
> Murdering impossibility, to make
> What cannot be, slight work.
>   (V, iii, 56–62)

We observe the cosmic imagery: we note the doctrine of
correspondences again. The claims of the order scheme assert
themselves in his mind, despite his powerful resolution to make
himself his own law. Even after seeing his mother kneeling to
him he tries to remain true to his isolationist vow. He begs
his mother not to ask him to dismiss his soldiers and give up
his enterprise against Rome. She has to plead. Ultimately
nature (in the order sense) prevails in Coriolanus, and he
learns self-sacrifice. He knows very well the danger to himself
which is involved in his sparing Rome. But, despite this,
nature prevails.

> O mother, mother!
> What have you done? Behold, the heavens do ope,
> The gods look down, and this unnatural scene
> They laugh at. O my mother, mother! O!
> You have won a happy victory to Rome;
> But, for your son,—believe it, O, believe it,
> Most dangerously you have with him prevail'd,
> If not most mortal to him. But, let it come.
>   (V, iii, 182–9)

We hear no more from Volumnia after this—not a word.
We are left with the impression of a noble woman who
(although herself once proud) has made a sacrifice for Rome—
for she has been told that her victory for Rome is for her
beloved son "most dangerous", perhaps "most mortal". *She*

has made a sacrifice in the name of nature: she has persuaded the hero to a great act of self-sacrifice in the name of nature.

Now Volumnia had previously persuaded Coriolanus to agree to sacrifice his pride in connection with his candidature for the consulship. But he simply could not carry the thing through properly. He spoke and acted in such a way as to bring upon himself the penalty of banishment. Volumnia's final endeavour at making him perform an act of self-sacrifice is indeed more successful. He refrains from sacking Rome and he remains true to that decision.

Volumnia's persuasions that he spare Rome have the effect of bringing about in Coriolanus a moral regeneration. It must be admitted that it is only a *partial* regeneration. Coriolanus spares Rome. But he has spoils to show for the expedition: and, returned to Corioli, he says:

> We have made peace
> With no less honour to the Antiates
> Than shame to the Romans.
>
> (V, vi, 79–81)

He tells Aufidius and the other Volscian lords that he has returned as their soldier,

> No more infected with my country's love
> Than when I parted hence.
>
> (V, vi, 72–3)

These are not the words of a man in whom nature (in the order sense) has been very firmly re-established! But remembering what has recently gone before we must say, I think, that here in Corioli we are looking on a man still proud, still egotistical, but for whom (if he survived) we could have hope. He has recently sunk his egotistical spirit of revenge sufficiently to make a concession to order: and, though this concession has been limited to an undertaking not to sack Rome, we feel that the hero has been proved to be a man who *can* get the better of the evil within him. He never does completely get the better of it. He never becomes fully reconciled to Rome. But even so we feel at the end, as his corpse is borne off the stage, that that partial moral regeneration was the most significant thing in his whole career: had he lived, the regeneration might perhaps ultimately have gone much further.

.   .   .   .   .

Let us now note a contrast between the patterns of *Macbeth* and *Coriolanus*. In *Macbeth* we start with the Witches: we start with external evil influences brought to bear on the hero. The hero has within him that seed of evil of which we have spoken: but it requires the external evil forces to bring it into active life, and its coming into active life is accompanied by a severe struggle in the hero between it and his order-value. Ultimately, however, evil triumphs in him; and in the end there is for him no regeneration. At his death order is restored in the environment, but not in Macbeth himself. In *Coriolanus* things are different. The hero stands forth from the start as proud and egotistical: the evil is active within him from the start without having to be called into life by any outside influence. The struggle within him between the claims of his egotism and the claims of order comes near the end, not as in *Macbeth* near the beginning: and the issue of the struggle is a degree of moral regeneration, not as in *Macbeth* the opposite. Thus the design of *Coriolanus* may be regarded as (at any rate in certain important respects) an inversion of the design of *Macbeth*, though both tragedies are concerned with the same order-disorder theme.

We have said that in *Coriolanus* no external force is necessary to bring to active life the evil that is in the hero's character. But it should be noted that he is *to some extent* a victim of others. Consider the following speech, delivered by Brutus, one of the tribunes:

> Go about it.
> Put him to choler straight: he hath been used
> Ever to conquer, and to have his worth
> Of contradiction: being once chafed, he cannot
> Be rein'd again to temperance; then he speaks
> What's in his heart; and that is there which looks
> With us to break his neck.
>
> (III, iii, 24–30)

The tribunes, anxious to ruin Coriolanus, are prepared deliberately to take advantage of Coriolanus's character—to

push him into endangering himself. To this extent Coriolanus
may be looked on as a victim of external compulsion. Yet it
must be said, I think, that of the two factors—Coriolanus's
self-responsibility, and compulsion from outside himself—the
former is presented by Shakespeare as very much the more
powerful. The factor of external compulsion is very much
weaker and less important than in *Macbeth* (or *Othello* or *King
Lear*), though it does exist. We feel that if Macbeth had never
met the Witches there would have been no tragedy at all: but
we feel, I think, that in all probability Coriolanus would in
any circumstances have ultimately come to grief.

A part of the design of *Coriolanus*, then, even if only a
small part, is that the tribunes victimize him. But on this
matter there is more to be said. What attitude are we supposed by Shakespeare to take up towards the tribunes—and
towards the plebs? The hero himself despises the plebs, and
addresses to them all manner of scurrilous speeches. Now it is
sometimes said that this is an anti-plebeian play—that Shakespeare means it to be that. But to say this seems to me to
betray a grave misunderstanding of what the play is essentially
about and a grave misunderstanding of what Shakespeare is,
in fact, saying in it.

The cardinal fact is that Coriolanus himself is portrayed as
proud, and his pride is not vindicated—the play itself condemns it. His manner of speaking to the plebs is part of his
pride—part of his unbalance, intemperance, disorder. Shakespeare is *not* saying to his audience that Coriolanus's attitude
to the commons is justifiable. The commons certainly have
legitimate grievances against the hero. Shakespeare is not
saying that the plebs should be allowed to make claims which
are contrary to the conception of hierarchy: he believes profoundly in the hierarchical structure of society, as of the whole
universe. And it is true that the commons are shown in the
play behaving at times in a vacillating and unworthy fashion.
But it is not part of Shakespeare's purpose in this play to get
his audience to say that it is dangerous to allow the plebs to
have their voice heard or to allow the plebs to have con-
stitutionally established officers to look after their interests.
Coriolanus is shown as erring in his attitude to the plebs. We

have said that the tribunes use machinations in order to get rid of him—they exploit his character in order to ruin him. That is true. At the same time these tribunes are not shown up in a consistently bad light by any means. They do not appear to wish to make any unwarrantable claims for those they represent. They are certainly not in favour of mob rule. After Coriolanus has been banished, Sicinius says:

> This is a happier and more comely time
> Than when these fellows ran about the streets,
> Crying confusion.
>
> (IV, vi, 27-9)

"These fellows" are the plebs. The tribunes are on the side of constitutional order. And immediately after the speech just quoted, the other tribune delivers a speech which we have already referred to, and he states no more nor less than the truth:

> Caius Marcius was
> A worthy officer i' the war; but insolent,
> O'ercome with pride, ambitious past all thinking,
> Self-loving,—
>
> (IV, vi, 29-32)

The tribunes may have been unscrupulous in exploiting Coriolanus's character in order to get rid of him: but they were exploiting what after all *was* in fact Coriolanus's character, and they were doing it in what they regarded as a good cause —they were intent on producing social justice. Shakespeare does *not* tell us that social justice demanded that the plebs continue to put up with Coriolanus's insults and intemperate pride. I have no doubt that the Shakespearian attitude was that the plebs should be ruled from above, but by wise and temperate rule, not by the kind of rule that Coriolanus approved of—repression with contumely.

. . . . .

Volumnia's pleading with him outside Rome induces the hero to perform an act of self-sacrifice. He allows the voice of nature (in the order sense) to subdue his pride to the extent of making him refrain from sacking Rome. He spares the city this fate, knowing that it may mean his own death. A man who, formerly vastly egotistical, risks his life for his native city[1] is a man morally regenerated. We have said, however, that Coriolanus is only partially regenerated. He returns to Corioli

> No more infected with my country's love
> Than when I parted hence.
>
> (V, vi, 72-3)

He tries to placate the Volscians. He does not seek out his own death at their hands to complete his act of self-sacrifice. He tries to avoid that. And his old personal pride is still there within him. Provoked by Aufidius, he speaks insultingly to him, and is so foolish[2] as to refer to his former achievements against the Volscians by whom he is now surrounded. This is the direct cause of his death—he is set upon and slain. He is never *fully* reclaimed from his egotism. But I think we may say that, in spite of this, Shakespeare leaves us with an impression of optimism. A consummate egotist *could* at a critical point allow order to prevail with him.

.   .   .   .   .

The fundamental order-disorder theme is to be found in all the tragedies, and the reader is recommended to consider them all in this light. Each play is, of course, a self-sufficient artistic entity, and my attempts to show that different plays have the same underlying theme are certainly not to be understood as a denial of this very important fact. The same basic theme is treated differently in different plays. But it is always there.

One final brief illustration. We have just spoken of *Coriolanus*. *Romeo and Juliet* presents a great contrast to *Coriolanus*, though again the order-disorder theme is cardinal in *Romeo and Juliet*. The obvious difference in design between the two plays is the difference between a "humour tragedy" and a tragedy of circumstance or fate. The troubles of Romeo and Juliet come upon them as a result of external circumstances.

---

[1] He had of course risked his life before as a warrior in the Roman army. But we may be sure that then he was at least largely concerned with his own fame. In sparing Rome he does not appear to be concerned with that.

[2] Throughout the play his pride entails lack of judgment.

It cannot be said that they themselves are to blame for their
fate. But I cannot treat this play at length: space forbids.
Suffice it to point out that the order-disorder theme is, as I
have said, cardinal in it. The love-story is set in a context of
social disorder. Conditions in Verona are virtually those of
civil war. We begin with this social disorder. And at the end
the unhappy fate of the lovers has the effect of healing the
disorder and bringing about order. The essential theme of the
play is stated at the outset in the prologue:

> Two households, both alike in dignity,
>   In fair Verona, where we lay our scene,
> From ancient grudge break to new mutiny,
>   Where civil blood makes civil hands unclean.
> From forth the fatal loins of these two foes
>   A pair of star-cross'd lovers take their life;
> Whose misadventured piteous overthrows
>   Do with their death bury their parents' strife.

Romeo and Juliet is not just a sad love story. It is a story dealing
essentially with the paradox that disorder is cured by the
unhappy outcome of a relationship which, in itself, deserved
to be happy. The Capulet-Montague disorder destroys the
lovers: the destruction of the lovers destroys the disorder, and
order results. That is essentially what the play is about.

CHAPTER VII

THE LAST PLAYS

WE have discussed comedies, histories, and tragedies. Now we have certain plays written by Shakespeare at the close of his career as a dramatist which are generally grouped together in a special category. These are three in number—*Cymbeline*, *The Winter's Tale*, and *The Tempest*. This group of plays, though it should, indeed, be separated from the other groups, is nevertheless basically concerned with the same ideas as we have discussed in connection with those other groups—they are concerned with disorder giving way to order. In this chapter we shall consider one of them by way of example: we shall consider *Cymbeline*. We shall trace the disorder-order pattern in it, and we shall also consider why it cannot be called a comedy or a tragedy (despite the fact that the first folio classifies it as a tragedy) but falls into a special category.

．　　　．　　　．　　　．　　　．

In *Cymbeline*, then, we have to do with a disordered environment and with the processes by which order is re-established. Evil is temporarily triumphant, but it ultimately gives way to good under providential guidance. For the state of disorder Cymbeline himself bears part of the initial responsibility. He makes two mistakes. First, he gives credence to the false witness of two villains who accuse Belarius of being a traitor, and so he banishes Belarius who is actually innocent of the charge. We may say that the two villains are part of the original disorder-situation: they bring their evil influence to bear on Cymbeline whose defective judgment ensures their success: and so Belarius is banished. This was some twenty years before the opening of the play. Second, immediately before the opening of the play Cymbeline has sentenced Posthumus to banishment. Posthumus has secretly married Cymbeline's daughter, Imogen. Cymbeline, apprised of this, banishes Posthumus. He may be said to have some justification for doing so. But it is an error of judgment, for Posthumus is an exceedingly fine man—just the sort of man that Cymbeline's kingdom needs.

The disorder in Cymbeline's kingdom is characterized by the same inversion as we found in *As You Like It* and elsewhere. Belarius was an honourable and valiant man who fought nobly for his king against invasion by the Romans. "My body's mark'd," he says,

> With Roman swords, and my report was once
> First with the best of note: Cymbeline loved me,
> And when a soldier was the theme, my name
> Was not far off.
>
> (III, iii, 56–60)

Yet it was for alleged confederacy with the Romans that he was banished. The inversion theme is stressed. Men of the court, engaged in warfare, seek out danger in the name of fame and honour which die "i' the search",

> And hath as oft a slanderous epitaph
> As record of fair act; nay, many times,
> Doth ill deserve by doing well.
>
> (III, iii, 51–54)

("Deserve" here means "earn".) In the disorder-environment one often earns bad treatment by doing good deeds. Compare Adam's words in *As You Like It:*

> Know you not, master, to some kind of men
> Their graces serve them but as enemies?

> O, what a world is this, when what is comely
> Envenoms him that bears it!
>
> (II, iii, 10–11, 14–15)

Shakespeare, then, emphasizes Belarius's moral uprightness before the banishment (for Belarius's words on this matter are for the information of the audience and are to be taken as true). He also emphasizes Posthumus's moral uprightness before his banishment. In the first scene of the play, in a conversation between two gentlemen, this is stressed: Posthumus, we are told,

> is a creature such
> As, to seek through the regions of the earth
> For one his like, there would be something failing
> In him that should compare.
>
> (I, i, 19–22)

And the speaker goes on:

> I do not think
> So fair an outward and such stuff within
> Endows a man but he.
>
> (I, i, 22–24)

This again is for the audience's information and is to be taken as true.

Now, subsequent to their bad treatment by Cymbeline, both Belarius and Posthumus themselves act wrongly. Consider the case of Belarius first. He takes revenge on Cymbeline by carrying off the latter's two sons and bringing them up in his place of exile, as his own sons, they being ignorant of their real rank. Now certainly this abduction is a crime. Belarius admits it. "Beaten for loyalty," he says, "Excited me to treason" (V, v, 344–5). He knows that it is treason, and his wrongdoing is deliberate. At the same time, we have the impression that he would not have committed it if Cymbeline had not acted unjustly towards him. That is to say, though Belarius cannot escape personal responsibility for his sin, that sin is in a sense a consequence of Cymbeline's wrongdoing. Cymbeline's wrongdoing was deliberately caused by the two villains. And so we have a chain of evil: the two villains, disorder-figures from the start, perverted Cymbeline—Cymbeline erred—and, as a consequence, Belarius, an upright man, turned into a wrongdoer. The two villains, we may say, have succeeded in turning good into bad.

We come now to Posthumus. On being banished he goes to Italy. In this play Shakespeare makes use of a view of Italy that was widespread in the England of his day—the view that Italy was a place where corruption flourished. Posthumus finds himself surrounded by an atmosphere of moral laxity.

And in Act I, scene v, in a conversation concerning feminine beauty and faithfulness, Posthumus, to quote R. G. Moulton,[1] "when the challenge is made that even [Imogen's] purity may be conquered, surrenders to the lower standard of morals around him, where virtue can be made a thing of wager and there is not capacity deep enough to take in perfection." And so Posthumus makes his wager with Iachimo, maintaining that Imogen will resist Iachimo's attack on her chastity. Posthumus's faith in Imogen, when he makes the bargain with Iachimo, is complete: he does not for a moment think that the temptation will put her in any danger. His intentions are in no way bad. Yet the audience is surely in no doubt that Posthumus is doing wrong in deliberately exposing her to temptation.

This wrongdoing of Posthumus leads in due course to Imogen's leaving her father Cymbeline's court; thus Cymbeline loses his daughter as he had before lost his two sons. The parallelism is deliberate and is part of the pattern of the play: Cymbeline banishes Belarius—as a direct result Belarius commits a wrong which robs Cymbeline of his sons; Cymbeline banishes Posthumus — as an indirect result Posthumus commits a wrong which ultimately robs Cymbeline of his daughter.

What are we to think of Iachimo? When he undertakes his mission to test Imogen's virtue we certainly feel that he is doing wrong. Yet we must allow, as Moulton maintains, that there is this to be said for him—he is, at first, genuinely anxious to prove what he regards as a truth, that even this paragon will be unfaithful, and that that is what woman's nature is. When Imogen repulses him, however, and his opinion is proved to be false, the character of his wrongdoing changes and he becomes a villain pure and simple, intent on destroying love and harmony: he becomes like the two villains who had slandered Belarius. He becomes an Iago-like figure.

As a result of this development in Iachimo, Posthumus's original wrongdoing is followed by more serious wrongdoing on his part. Iachimo returns to him with a false story,

[1] *The Moral System of Shakespeare* (1903), p. 79.

bolstered up by what seems convincing evidence. Posthumus believes Iachimo's story (just as Cymbeline had believed the two villains), and he sends directions to his servant Pisanio to kill Imogen. He believes that his directions are carried out, and in the later portions of the play he is deeply remorseful.

It will be seen that the various pieces of wrongdoing in the play form a connected tissue of evil. One error or sin seems to beget another. And it should be noted too that, as Moulton says, "the separate trains of evil are drawn into a unity by the way in which they one and all strike at Imogen. Through the error of Cymbeline," he continues, "Imogen has lost her husband, through the retaliation of Belarius she has lost her brothers; Posthumus's sin robs her of her love, and the crime of Iachimo robs her of her reputation; by the queen her life is threatened, and the villainy of Cloten threatens her honour. In the sequel all these are saved or restored, and Imogen appears a motive centre for the whole of this many-sided plot: in her the lines of complication meet, and her sufferings are foremost among the forces of resolution."[1]

These evils, present in Cymbeline's kingdom, indicate that that kingdom is in a state of thorough moral corruption: and this corruption results in the fact that Cymbeline's forces, fighting against the Romans, are initially defeated dishonourably, Cymbeline himself being captured.

Now in the play we find, presented *in extenso*, the process of regeneration, restoration of order, moral rehabilitation. In studying it, let us begin by noting the significance of the scenes that take place in the Welsh mountains, Belarius's place of exile.

Belarius contrasts life in the Welsh mountains with life in the court, in a way that reminds us of the contrast between the forest of Arden and the court in *As You Like It*. The contrast is expressed in the very first speech in the first of the mountain scenes. Belarius says:

> A goodly day not to keep house, with such
> Whose roof's as low as ours! Stoop, boys; this gate
> Instructs you how to adore the heavens and bows you

[1] Op. cit., p. 84.

> To a morning's holy office: the gates of monarchs
> Are arch'd so high that giants may jet through
> And keep their impious turbans on, without
> Good morrow to the sun. Hail, thou fair heaven!
> We house i' the rock, yet use thee not so hardly
> As prouder livers do.
>   (III, iii, 1–9)

Those who live in this mountain retreat exemplify a natural piety which those who live in courts do not. A moment or two later we have Belarius saying that this simple mountain life "is nobler than attending for a check" (i.e., awaiting a command) and "prouder than rustling in unpaid-for silk". The courtier's life is "no life to ours", no life in comparison with this one. He speaks feelingly of "the city's usuries", and of "the art o' the court",

> As hard to leave as keep; whose top to climb
> Is certain falling, or so slippery that
> The fear's as bad as falling.
>   (III, iii, 47–49)

Those who live in the mountains need fear no poison "which attends in place of greater state". The court is the place where people are treated as Belarius was treated by Cymbeline— where malice, envy, slander, infidelity, ingratitude, treachery flourish: amid the mountains the virtues of the inhabitants have full sway and there is no unnaturalness. Just as in the forest of Arden, so in the Welsh mountains, the inhabitants have to put up with physical hardship. But their physical and moral health amply compensate for that. "Come," says Belarius, "our stomachs" (i.e. appetites)

> Will make what's homely savoury: weariness
> Can snore upon the flint, when resty sloth
> Finds the down pillow hard.
>   (III, vi, 32–35)

The mountain people scorn gold and silver: gold and silver are considered better than dirt only by those who "worship dirty gods", as they do in the city.

Belarius's refuge in the Welsh mountains, then, is another forest of Arden: we have the same physical hardship and moral

N

health, and the same contrast with a corrupt court milieu.
There is no doubt that we are meant by Shakespeare to take
this favourable view of the Welsh mountain life. Cymbeline's
two sons, Guiderius and Arviragus, have been brought up
here, and their characters have been partly shaped by conditions here—we are certainly meant to understand that.
But just as in *As You Like It*, so here, we find that the rural
retreat is not to be accepted as a refuge from court life for
ever and ever. Its function is to nurture in moral health those
who will bring regeneration to the corrupt court environment.

When we, the audience, get to Belarius's home we find
that Guiderius and Arviragus feel restricted, confined, frustrated here, and long to go down into the world of men.
They are critics of the mountain life—we had critics of the
forest life in *As You Like It*. To Belarius, Guiderius says:

> we, poor unfledged,
> Have never wing'd from view o' the nest, nor know not
> What air's from home . . .

> (III, iii, 27–29)

(i.e. what the air is like away from our home). "Haply,"
Guiderius says,

> this life is best,
> If quiet life be best; sweeter to you
> That have a sharper known; well corresponding
> With your stiff age: but unto us it is
> A cell of ignorance; travelling a-bed;
> A prison for a debtor, that not dares
> To stride a limit . . .

> (III, iii, 29–35)

(i.e. to go outside the restricted area that the authorities have
allowed him). And Arviragus has his say, too:

> We have seen nothing;
> We are beastly, subtle as the fox for prey,
> Like warlike as the wolf for what we eat;
> Our valour is to chase what flies; our cage
> We make a quire, as doth the prison'd bird,
> And sing our bondage freely.

> (III, iii, 39–44)

The longing of the youths to leave their mountain home is explained by the fact that, scions of the royal stock (although they do not know it), they have inherited the temper of royalty, and instinctively want to be doing the deeds that noble-hearted princes should do. This theme of the importance of heredity in determining temperament is explicitly treated by Belarius: speaking in soliloquy about the two youths, he says:

> They think they are mine; and though train'd up thus meanly
> I' the cave wherein they bow, their thoughts do hit
> The roofs of palaces, and nature prompts them
> In simple and low things to prince it much
> Beyond the trick of others.

> (III, iii, 82–86)

And later on he says:

> 'Tis wonder
> That an invisible instinct should frame them
> To royalty unlearn'd, honour untaught,
> Civility not seen from other.

> (IV, ii, 176–79)

In connection with Guiderius and Arviragus, then, we must keep a balance between two factors—(i) as sons of the king (though ignorant of the fact) they are instinctively drawn to the life that princes should lead—they want to leave the seclusion of the mountains—and we feel that it is a completely legitimate desire; but (ii) they have actually been brought up in the mountains, and this has had a beneficial formative effect upon them.

The two youths finally do come down from the mountains into the world of men; and they play an important part in the regenerative process which forms the latter part of the play. In his fight against the Romans, Cymbeline at first does badly; as we have seen, his army is routed and he himself taken captive. We feel that the moral corruption of the kingdom has a bearing on the poor performance of his army. But then the situation is saved; and the valour of these kingly youths from the mountains is one of the things that help to save it. They fight bravely and help to win the battle and reinstate Cymbeline. Here we have Nature as a re-integrating force in a double sense: for, as we have said, Nature has influenced the youths in their daily life in the mountain fastness, and at the same time Nature has preserved in them their noble hereditary disposition.

Nature, this restorative force, working on Guiderius and Arviragus, works also through them on Belarius. For he too fights valiantly and helps to restore Cymbeline's position. In doing so, he expiates his sin of long ago in stealing the two boys away—that is, he cancels out his own disorder. And we note that what drives him to assist in the regenerating process is the influence upon him of the enthusiasm of the two boys— Nature working on him through them.

There are other restorative influences which should be mentioned. Just as the evil in the play is a complex tissue, so the substitution of good for evil is achieved by a variety of means. Posthumus is overtaken by deep remorse for the wrong he has done, and his remorse induces him to play a part in righting the wrong. Iachimo also repents and confesses the evil he has done, his confession contributing to the happy conclusion. We may say that in both these cases natural feeling re-establishes itself in the hearts of former wrongdoers, and this contributes to the restoration of order, harmony, and virtue in the world of the play. Nor should we forget the figures of Pisanio and the physician Cornelius, whose conduct is such as to help to frustrate the evil intentions of villainy. By means of all these restorative forces with which we have dealt, all becomes well in the end.

I think it is true to say that as we read or watch the play we have a strong impression that the process of restoration is presided over by an actively beneficent Providence. Thus, for example, we have emphasized that when Guiderius and Arviragus come down from the mountains and take part in the restoration process they do not know who they really are— they do not in fact know what they are really doing. We may say that we have Nature itself as an active re-integrating force, working through these characters who are to some extent its passive instruments. And we feel more than this: we feel that it is Providence which is making use of Nature in this way. The over-riding providential factor in the play, implicit throughout, is made explicit in prophetic visions (see IV, ii, 346; V, v, 426 and 467) and in the masque.

I would quote Moulton again: "The masque introduced into the play of *Cymbeline* is simply a dramatization of providence, Jove and the gods descending to read the meaning of dark dispensations. It may," he goes on, "be a question how much of this masque is genuine. But as it stands it unites with other parts of the play in that which, more than anything else, emphasizes the providence underlying the whole plot—the emergence from time to time of great principles of moral government. When to Pisanio the drift of events is at its darkest he is made to appeal to a higher power: 'The heavens still must work'. And again,

> All other doubts by time let them be clear'd:
> Fortune brings in some boats that are not steer'd.

The deity of the masque gives comfort against the 'mortal accidents' that have befallen Posthumus:

> Whom best I love I cross; to make my gift,
> The more delay'd, delighted . . .
> He shall be lord of lady Imogen,
> And happier much by his affliction made.

And in the sorest strait to which Imogen is brought in her wanderings, words are spoken to her which may well stand as foundation principle of the whole plot: 'Some falls are means the happier to arise'."[1] It is the reverse of the Falls of Princes theme.

If the reader studies *The Winter's Tale* and *The Tempest* he will find plenty of reasons for acquiescing in the classification of these two plays along with *Cymbeline* as a definite connected group. There are plenty of corresponding features. To take only one example, the significance of the Welsh mountains in *Cymbeline* is matched by that of the pastoral Bohemian scenes in *The Winter's Tale*—in both cases we have a sequestered region of rural innocence as the place where restorative force is nurtured so that it may be subsequently brought to bear on the corrupt world of men which it is to cleanse. And the island of *The Tempest* is the same thing. The reader is recommended to study all three plays together.

[1] Op. cit., pp. 87-8.

Unfortunately in this little volume we have not the space to
do so.

There is a famous critical pronouncement by Lytton
Strachey with which our analysis of *Cymbeline* must force us
to disagree emphatically. Lytton Strachey believed that in his
last plays Shakespeare was getting bored. "It is difficult,"
says Strachey, "to resist the conclusion that Shakespeare was
getting bored himself. Bored with people, bored with real
life, bored with drama, bored, in fact, with everything except
poetry and poetical dreams. He is no longer interested, one
often feels, in what happens, or who says what, so long as he
can find place for a faultless lyric, or a new, unimagined
rhythmical effect, or a grand and mystic speech."[1] None can
deny, of course, the lyricism of the new rhythmic effects or
the grand mystic speeches: none can deny the strange new
music of the last plays. But to say that that is all there is to
them is simply nonsense. What is true of *Cymbeline* is true of
the whole group; and in *Cymbeline* we have a coherent dramatic
structure which embodies the expression of a view of life which
is very "real"—Shakespeare is here vitally concerned with
actual life and with the providential force which ultimately
controls it. He is certainly not bored with people or with real
life or with drama. *Cymbeline* is full of interesting people: it is
a play about real life and its deepest realities—order and disorder, good and evil, Nature, Providential control: and it has
a remarkably well conducted complex dramatic shape.

.   .   .   .   .

The three last plays are sometimes called "romances";
and they are sometimes called "tragi-comedies". It is legitimate
to call them romances, though, of course, there is romance in
plenty in other plays as well—what are *As You Like It* and
Twelfth Night, for example, if not romances? For the plays
with which we are here concerned the term "romances",
suitable in itself, is perhaps hardly exclusive enough. It
may be suggested that the term "tragi-comedies" is better.
The emotional reaction called forth by these three plays,
Cymbeline, *The Winter's Tale*, and *The Tempest*, in places

[1] See Tillyard, *Shakespeare's Last Plays* (1938), p. 2.

approaches the kind of emotional reaction called forth by the tragedies—and it is not just a matter of an isolated moment, as at the point in *Much Ado About Nothing* where Beatrice says "Kill Claudio". But the restoration of order has about it a different atmosphere from that of the tragedies—it resembles rather that of the comedies. Let us look at this a little more closely.

In his book, *Shakespeare's Last Plays*, Dr. Tillyard relates the pattern of these plays to that of the tragedies in a way which I think is excellent. He points out (and I take it that this is agreed by all teachers) that the tragedies end on a note of restoration of order and virtue, a note of reconciliation, re-integration, regeneration. In each case we feel that order is restored—evil has been overcome by good. But, as Dr. Tillyard notes, in the tragedies the regeneration is not treated at length—it is not treated on the scale on which the antecedent disintegration was treated. The restoration of order in *Macbeth* or *King Lear* is, as it were, just the finishing touch to the drama. Dr. Tillyard advances the theory, which I think is correct, that "one of Shakespeare's main concerns in his last plays, whether deliberately taken up or fortuitously drifted into, was to develop the final phase of the tragic pattern."[1]

What we have in *Cymbeline*, for example, is a play embodying the tragic pattern with the regenerative process treated more fully than in the tragedies. We have used the term "tragi-comedies". The first element of this compound term is justified by the fact that the plays show a state of disorder in such a way that we feel it is a serious matter—more serious than the disorder we see in the comedies. Our emotional reaction to it is closer to our reaction to disorder in the tragedies than to our reaction to disorder in the comedies. But Shakespeare concentrates our attention predominantly in these plays on the reintegrational process, so that we feel that we are not really in the realm of tragedy—the keynote, to put the matter rather over-simply, is too optimistic.

In the tragedies we feel that Shakespeare's attention is predominantly fixed on the terrible fact of disintegration—at the end there is regeneration, certainly, but at a dreadful cost.

[1] Op. cit., p. 20.

BOOK LIST

The works mentioned in the body of the present volume are not included in the following list. Unfortunately, many other valuable works must also be omitted from the list; for our space is limited, and the number of books that have been written about Shakespeare and his plays is tremendous. Again, some valuable works have been published since the manuscript of the present volume was completed.

ALEXANDER, PETER. *Shakespeare's Life and Art*. London, Nisbet, 1939.

BOAS, F. S. *Shakespeare and his Predecessors*. London, John Murray, 1896.

BRADBROOK, M. C. *Elizabethan Stage Conditions*. Cambridge University Press, 1932.

BRADBY, ANNE. *Shakespeare Criticism, 1919–35*. Oxford University Press (World's Classics), 1936.

BRADLEY, A. C. *Oxford Lectures on Poetry*. London, Macmillan, 1909.

BROWN, IVOR. *Shakespeare*. London, Collins, 1949.

CAMPBELL, LILY B. *Shakespeare's Tragic Heroes*. Cambridge University Press, 1930.

CHAMBERS, E. K. *Sources for a Biography of Shakespeare*. Oxford, Clarendon Press, 1946.

CHARLTON, H. B. *Shakespearian Comedy*. London, Methuen, 1938.

COWLING, GEORGE H. *A Preface to Shakespeare*. London, Methuen, 1925.

GRANVILLE-BARKER, HARLEY. *Prefaces to Shakespeare*. 5 vols. London, Sidgwick and Jackson, 1927 onwards.
    and HARRISON, G. B. (editors). *A Companion to Shakespeare Studies*. Cambridge University Press, 1934.

HARBAGE, ALFRED. *Shakespeare's Audience*. Columbia University Press, 1941.
As They Liked It. An Essay on Shakespeare and Morality. New York, Macmillan Co., 1947.

HARRISON, G. B. *Shakespeare at Work*. London, Routledge, 1933.
Elizabethan Plays and Players. London, Routledge, 1940.

HERFORD, C. H. *A Study of Recent Shakespearean Investigation, 1893–1923*. London, Blackie, 1923.

LAWRENCE, W. J. *Shakespeare's Workshop*. Oxford, Blackwell, 1928.
Those Nut-Cracking Elizabethans. London, Argonaut Press, 1935.

LAWRENCE, W. W. *Shakespeare's Problem Comedies*. New York, Macmillan Co., 1931.

MACCALLUM, M. W. *Shakespeare's Roman Plays*. London, Macmillan, 1910.

MACKAIL, J. W. *The Approach to Shakespeare*. Oxford, Clarendon Press, 1933.

MASEFIELD, JOHN. *William Shakespeare*. London, Williams and Norgate (Home University Library), 1911.

MOULTON, R. G. *Shakespeare as a Dramatic Artist*. Oxford, Clarendon Press, 1885.

NICOLL, ALLARDYCE. *Studies in Shakespeare*. London, Hogarth Press, 1927.

PALMER, JOHN. *Political Characters of Shakespeare*. London, Macmillan, 1945.
Comic Characters of Shakespeare. London, Macmillan, 1946.

PARROTT, T. M. *Shakespearean Comedy*. Oxford University Press, 1949.

QUILLER-COUCH, ARTHUR. *Shakespeare's Workmanship*. London, Benn, 1918.

RALEIGH, WALTER. *Shakespeare*. London, Macmillan (English Men of Letters Series), 1907.

SMITH, D. NICHOL. *Shakespeare Criticism, a Selection*. Oxford University Press (World's Classics), 1916.

SMITH, L. PEARSALL. *On Reading Shakespeare*. London, Constable, 1933.

SPENS, JANET. *An Essay on Shakespeare's Relation to Tradition*. Oxford, Blackwell, 1916.

SPRAGUE, A. C. *Shakespeare and the Audience*. Harvard University Press, 1935.

STEVENSON, D. L. *The Love-Game Comedy*. Columbia University Press, 1946.

STEWART, J. I. M. *Character and Motive in Shakespeare*. London, Longmans, 1949.

STOLL, E. E. *Shakespeare and Other Masters*. Harvard University Press, 1940.

TILLYARD, E. M. W. *Shakespeare's Problem Plays*. Toronto University Press, 1949.

VAN DOREN, MARK. *Shakespeare*. New York, Holt, 1939.

WILLIAMS, CHARLES. *A Short Life of Shakespeare. With the Sources. Abridged from Sir Edmund Chambers's "William Shakespeare."* Oxford, Clarendon Press, 1933.

WILSON, J. DOVER. *The Essential Shakespeare*. Cambridge University Press, 1937.

INDEX